D0208774

Faith Teaching

Teachers *Like You* Can Grow Faith Kids

by
Steve Wamberg
and John Conaway

Foreword by
Norm Wright

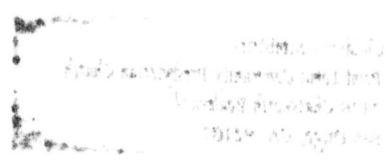

Faith Teaching

Teachers *Like You* Can Grow Faith Kids

Editor: Doug Schmidt
Cover design: Image Studios

About the authors:
With over 50 years of church ministry experience between them, Steve Wamberg and John Conaway write as church "insiders"—people who love God, His church, and His people. Steve is an ordained minister who also has experience as a curriculum writer, musician, puppeteer, church renewal specialist, and Sunday school teacher. John first became involved in church ministry by helping his missionary mother handle Sunday school flannelgraphs when he was six years old. Since then he has served in most volunteer church positions at one time or another—especially teaching Sunday school—and for over 20 years has worked as a full-time curriculum developer. And most importantly, as family men, Steve and John are deeply committed to strong links between church and home.

Table of Contents

Foreword
by Norm Wright

I am delighted to contribute to this project by writing a foreword.

Having been involved as a Christian Educator for over thirty-eight years, my concern is still focused on what transpires between church teaching and home.

After reading *Faith Teaching*, my response was, "Yes! Teachers can still impact the lives of their students in a practical way!" Not only that, but there is even greater emphasis upon church/ home involvement than when I began ministry in the early 1960s. (That does sound ancient, doesn't it?)

This resource is carefully crafted and insightfully tied into the everyday life of the student. It is also easy to read—the realistic dialogue takes the readers into the Sunday school experience in such a way that they will come away with the response, "Yes, I can do that."

Any teacher will find this book a helpful resource and will return to it time and time again for ideas, inspiration, and encouragement.

I would encourage every church school worker, as well as Christian school teachers, to devour this resource.

H. Norman Wright
Author and
Marriage, Family & Child Counselor

Introduction

THERE HAS ALWAYS BEEN A COMMON LINK between Sunday school and the home: the student. When the student is prepared to take his faith home and to examine his world through the faith he learns with others at church, miracles happen.

What was the last miracle in your Sunday school class?

"Okay, so we have 12 calendar pads, 12 picture frames, and—wait a minute—13 pictures. Did we get a new student last week? What's up with this?"

"Hold on. Let me see." Jeri took the stack of pictures from Norm. "By the way, you need to pack a couple extra calendars and frames, just in case we have visitors this week."

"That's why I'm here—to put your wisdom into action, sweetheart."

Norm finished packing the box of craft materials with the extras included. He almost hated to admit it, but he actually looked forward to Sunday mornings and team teaching the elementary class with his wife, Jeri. Their own children were in college. He'd forgotten how invigorating an eight year old's perspective on God and the world could be—and he got a kick out of hearing their "zingers" in the classroom.

The kids loved Norm, too. Some of them even called him "Grandpa Norm." (He'd warned them about calling Jeri "Grandma" just yet. "Mrs. Mills" would have to do for a while.)

Jeri looked up from the pictures and sighed deeply. "I forgot— it's the first Christmas since the Rikers split up. We have two pictures here of Ryan."

Norm's face fell. "Crying shame, that is . . . Did anyone ever figure out what was up with Rick?"

"No, just a lot of speculation. Carol doesn't even seem to know."

"So he didn't buy a red convertible and take off with his secretary?"

"Apparently not. One week he was there, the next week he was gone. I understand that he said something to his small group about 'needing his space' and 'finding himself.' "

"Weren't we supposed to have taken motorcycle trips to the desert when we were 19 years old to do that stuff? Wasn't he thinking about his kids?"

Introduction

"Norm, I'm just telling you what I've heard."

"Well, I'll make it a point to stay close to Ryan tomorrow."

The next morning seemed bright for late December. Norm stayed within arm's length of Ryan during the opening song time, and kept his hand on the boy's shoulder as they made their way to the classroom.

"Hey Grandpa Norm, Dad's picking me up after Sunday school today. We're going to spend New Year's together and watch the football games at his apartment. Just us guys! Pretty cool, huh?"

"Guess so, little buddy." Norm managed a weak smile. Ryan was making the best of things. Norm figured he owed it to him to show a little positive attitude about the situation.

The Sunday school lesson revolved around Psalm 90:12:

Teach us to number our days aright,

that we may gain a heart of wisdom.

The children talked about what they'd do if they could do anything they wanted in a single day. They covered the kinds of fun they'd have, who they'd have it with, and what they'd change.

Ryan joined right in the discussion. His hand shot up and he said matter-of-factly, "If I could do anything I wanted today, I'd make my Dad move back in with us."

At their age, the kids around the table didn't know how to have a moment of social embarrassment for Ryan. Instead, Kevin piped up, "Yeah, Ryan. I'd hate it if my mom and dad weren't together." The other kids nodded in agreement.

Jeri started distributing craft supplies. "Right now, to help us learn our memory verses, let's make a calendar to give to your parents. Think of it as a New Year's gift. Choose a piece of construction paper you like for the background of the calendar. In the upper left hand corner, write today's memory verse as neatly as you can. Then . . ."

Norm knew how the calendar was supposed to go together. He rifled through the stack of student pictures and handed each student his or her picture—two for Ryan.

"Looks like you have double duty here, Ryan. Let me know if I can help you, OK?"

"Sure, Grandpa Norm." Ryan twisted his tongue in his cheek to keep the memory verse printed in the limited space he wanted. "I think I can handle it."

In a few moments, the verses were written, the calendars and frames glued together, and the pictures inserted. The class finished by brainstorming ways the students could make the most of the new year. "Study harder!" "Watch less TV!" "Do better at obeying my parents!" "Read my Bible more!" "Get a watch!"

"Get a watch?" Norm smiled at Kevin.

"Sure! How can you number days the right way if you don't even know what time it is?"

"Good point!"

Jeri asked the students to privately choose one thing they would do this coming week to use their time wisely. "Next Sunday, we'll talk about how we did!"

The class ended in prayer, and the kids scurried off to the

church service—everyone but Ryan.

For a minute, Ryan busied himself in helping Norm and Jeri pick up the leftover craft supplies. Then he sat down and put his head in his hands. Norm and Jeri stopped what they were doing. Jeri sat in a chair beside him. Norm knelt down and gently patted Ryan's shoulder.

"What's up, buddy?"

Ryan looked up. He looked upset, but he wasn't letting himself cry. "Do you think my dad will ever come home?"

"I don't know the answer to that, Ryan. Wish I did." Norm let a few seconds pass before speaking again. "But can we pray with you about that? Let's ask God to bring your dad back home."

Kids' prayers are the best, because they cut to the chase right away. "God, I need my dad at home. So does Mom. So do my brothers. Bring him home, willya please? Please, Jesus?"

Norm nodded. "Please, Father. We agree with Ryan's prayer."

Jeri was getting weepy. "Oh, yes, Heavenly Father. Please answer this prayer for us." Then she put her arms around Ryan and hugged him.

"Mrs. Mills, do you need a Kleenex? I have an extra one rolled up in my pocket."

"No thanks, Ryan," Jeri smiled, wiping her eyes. "I'm okay."

"Well, Dad's waiting for me. I gotta go now." Ryan took his two calendars—one for each parent—and stood up to leave.

Norm walked with Ryan to the front of the church. He didn't know why, but he was rather surprised to see Rick waiting there at the curb. He waved at Rick. When Ryan saw his dad, he started running toward him. Rick got out of the driver's seat and came around to the passenger's side in time to scoop Ryan up in a bear hug. Norm watched Ryan and Rick settle into the car and drive off. "Please, Father. Bring him home."

The next Sunday Jeri opened class by asking, "How did your parents like their New Year's calendars?"

It's nearly impossible to make a craft featuring a child's picture that isn't a hit with parents. This one was no exception.

"My dad said he was going to keep it on his desk at work," Ryan added with a hint of pride.

Hope it takes. Norm kept the thought to himself, but made it a point to add Rick to his prayer list.

Jeri's second question officially started the class. "Last week we decided to do something to use our time more wisely. Who wants to talk about what happened?"

It was March when Norm and Jeri had early visitors to their Sunday school class. Ryan walked through the door beaming.

Rick and Carol were on either side of him, holding his hands.

"We need to thank you." The words were not coming easily from Rick.

Norm and Jeri furrowed their brows together almost in unison. Jeri finally spoke up. "For what?"

"Hey Ryan, go check on your brothers for a minute. Make sure they're sitting where they need to be."

"Okay, Dad!" Norm hadn't seen Ryan this relaxed for months.

"The calendars . . . the New Year's calendars. I'd look at mine every day at work. I'd see Ryan, I'd see the verse, and I started missing my family. There was no way I was spending my time wisely being apart from them." Rick looked at the floor.

Carol jumped in, "And when he asked to come back, I was ready to let him suffer and beg to see if he really meant it." Norm could see where Ryan got his matter-of-fact approach to hard times. "But that wouldn't have been a wise use of time either—and I've been reminded of that every day this year."

"We're not out of the woods yet. We've got a lot to work out, especially me. We start meeting with Pastor this Tuesday. But we'll be working it out together. So . . . thanks. Really."

Norm cleared his throat. "You know Ryan's been praying for this for quite a while."

"Yeah. So have you. Ryan's your biggest fan." Rick reached over to shake Norm's hand.

"Right now, we are too." Carol hugged Jeri. "Thanks for being here for him—and for us."

Faith Teaching

This miracle you just read about is a true story. We changed the names and a few details. As of this writing, we don't know whether Rick and Carol have completely worked things through. But they're still working at their issues as a family. Rick, Carol, and Ryan alike are quite convinced that God uses Sunday school to help families like theirs.

We're convinced too. You see, the church and the home have a lot in common: some very important people and a very important mission. The *people* are the students—children, teenagers, adults—who are both a part of a home and a part of a Sunday school class. The *mission* shared by church and home is to grow those students into deeper faith. The shared people and mission make up what we call the church/home link. The good news for you is that *the link already exists!* All you need to do is learn how to use it more effectively.

How can we strengthen the church/home link?

This isn't a new question. Over 125 years ago, a number of churches thought the answer was *common lesson content*. The thinking was that the best way to do Christian education was for every age level to study the same Scripture passage on the same Sunday. People who were visiting in another church wouldn't miss a Sunday school lesson, and all members of the family would have something in common to talk about after Sunday school. To accomplish this well-intentioned goal, outlines for the International Sunday School Lessons were created, and are still published to this day by the Committee on the Uniform Series of the National Council of Churches. Many mainline churches use curriculums that follow those outlines. And from time to time, other publishers have come up with their own variation on uniform lessons, in which all ages study the same lesson from the same Bible passage.

Though common (or uniform) lesson content sounds like a good idea at first, many Christian educators point out some serious inadequacies in this approach. First, if every age level studies the same Bible passage age-appropriately, will they really be learning the same lesson? There's a lot of difference between the way a six year old and a thirty-six year old understand the same Bible events. (For a more detailed treatment of "appropriateness," see Chapter 11.) Second, if the outlines include only those Scripture passages that all can understand the same way, what parts of the Bible—out of necessity—will be skipped? Books like Romans, which require mature thinking skills, are beyond the understanding of preschoolers; yet youth and adults need to have their thinking stretched beyond the concrete stories that are appropriate for young children. (By the way, even the Uniform Series lessons frequently suggest different lesson topics—and even different Scripture passages—for children, youth, and adults!)

So if common content isn't the answer to linking church and home, what is? Well, like many things in life, it's a lot simpler—and a lot more profound—than you might think. The church and the home fulfill different but equally important roles in growing people of faith. The role of the church is something we call Faith Teaching—the subject of this book. The role of the home is Faith Parenting.

Here's a working definition of Faith Teaching: *Faith Teaching is the process the church uses to develop "faith kids" by helping them learn and apply Bible truth to their lives. This teaching usually follows an intentional plan and takes place in a more structured environment than the home.*

The purpose of this book is to broaden your understanding of Faith Teaching and increase your appreciation of its importance. (We'll also talk a lot about "faith kids.") Through stories, illustrations, and practical principles, you'll see how you're already succeeding in your Faith Teaching role. We'll also suggest some ideas that can help you do it even better. (If you're a parent, you'll also want to read *Faith Parenting*, the companion book to this one.)

At the bottom line, you—as a Faith Teacher—represent the church side of the church/home link. Teachers like you walk alongside parents in nurturing faith in their children. Teachers like you keep parents informed about what you're teaching their children, even by simply placing take-home papers in the hands of the kids as they leave your classroom. Teachers like you encourage your students to take what they've learned and somehow apply it throughout the week.

Of course, it's always a plus when the Sunday school materials you're using actually encourage Faith Teaching. So along the way, we'll offer you a few guidelines for evaluating curriculum, too.

Introduction

As you begin reading this book, ask yourself this question: Do you see the parents and families of your students as your partners in nurturing the faith growth of your students? If so, you've already taken the crucial first step in becoming a Faith Teacher. The God who called you to teach Sunday school will give you what you need to take the next step . . . and then the one after that.

May God bless you as you explore this exciting subject with us.

Steve Wamberg
John Conaway
Colorado Springs, Colorado

What's a Faith Kid?

A "FAITH KID" IS A PERSON OF ANY AGE who responds to a faith relationship with God through Jesus Christ—and continues to grow in that relationship.

In other words, faith kids are people (even adults) who somehow show Jesus is alive and well in their hearts, minds, and actions—no matter what their age, no matter where they are in life.

Know any?

It had been a long road for young Jamie, and no one felt it exactly the way Don did.

Ten short years ago Don had been coaching Jamie in little league soccer. The kid's enthusiasm made up for the skills he lacked at first. Then Jamie's learning curve—a short one, at that—kicked in. Jamie was not only the team's most improved player that year, but also ended up as its leading scorer. Combined with his smarts in school and the musical gifts Jamie had inherited from his parents, the future looked dazzling.

The dazzle diminished the next year, when the strength began to leave Jamie's legs. The diagnosis was something that Don still couldn't pronounce properly. But no one could miss its effects on Jamie. A painfully gradual process of atrophy set in. The disease had taken its sweet time going from Jamie's legs to his shoulders to his torso. Then, over a few more years, it robbed Jamie of most of his ability to communicate. He could raise eyebrows, blink, and mumble. That was about it.

But whatever words Jamie did get out were golden. That's why Don encouraged Jamie's parents to keep bringing him to Sunday school.

Six years before, Don had seen Jamie commit his life to Jesus—as best any eight year old could. At the same service Don's son, Mark, also made such a commitment. That decision set loose a whirlwind in the Christian education department of their church. Jamie's mind was like a steel trap. He caught details from Bible stories, and sometimes even sermons, that kept the adults around him shaking their heads in wonder. Jamie came up with some questions that were really corkers, and built a reputation for keeping his classmates—and his teachers—on their toes.

Jamie's faith wasn't limited to his mind, either. This kid,

maybe because of his illness, knew that Jesus was his ultimate hope. There wasn't a doctor, nurse, therapist, or playmate—Mark among them—who didn't know about Jamie's relationship with Jesus. Jamie's growing confidence and trust in God, even as he watched his own body fall apart, was simply amazing.

As the disease limited Jamie's movement in the next few years, he became a chaplain of sorts to his peers. They came to him with questions and Jamie usually delivered just the right encouragement. When Jamie became less verbal, his friends still came to him just to unload. They knew they had Jamie's ear, and Jamie thrived on the interaction.

Jamie moved from a walker to a wheelchair the summer before he entered the high school class that Don taught. Don thought long and hard about the dilemma that posed: the high school classroom was located up a long flight of stairs. It was placed there, at the end of one wing of the building, because the location allowed for a livelier discussion and more activity. The high school room had couches instead of chairs and tables. The artists of the class repainted the classroom walls in a new mural every school year. The students "coming up" from middle school really looked forward to Sunday school in the high school room.

But what about Jamie?

The Sunday before the transition, Jamie's parents, Stan and Ellen, approached Don about the problem. "Listen, Coach." (Stan still called Don "Coach" from the little league soccer days.) "We know Jamie's going to have trouble getting up the stairs to the high school class. We can't carry the wheelchair up there, and you shouldn't have to, either."

"Well, I've been thinking about asking for a classroom switch."

"But the room is so important to the teenagers. It's important to Jamie, just because of the 'high school mystique' and the furniture and all. You shouldn't have to change everything for Jamie . . ." Ellen's voice faded toward the end. "We're thinking we might just take Jamie home before Sunday school."

"Please. Let me talk to the kids before you make that decision. Just give me today. Please."

Stan and Ellen shrugged. "Okay, Coach." Stan turned to watch Jamie making his way toward them from a conversation with two of his friends. "Just let us know. We're on our way to Grandma's today, but we'll be home this evening. Right, Sport?"

"Better . . . be!" Jamie's tone was firm, but his eyes were twinkling.

Stan explained, "Jamie wants to get back in time to watch a soccer game on TV, and Grandma doesn't have any sports channels. Talk to you later, Coach."

Don went by the middle school class and asked the teacher to bring her students to the high school room. The high schoolers were waiting for Don when he walked in with the entire middle school class.

"Whoa! An invasion!" A soon-to-be senior won cheers with his keen analysis.

"Just temporary. We'll send them back in a few minutes so they can enjoy Sunday school in peace." Don called the kids to order. "I want to talk to you about a friend of ours. Jamie's in a wheelchair now."

"Yeah, we noticed. For how long?"

Leave it to a teenager to go for the jugular. Don worked his mouth from side to side before talking. "Probably for the rest of his life." A hush fell over the kids.

"Here's the problem: Jamie's parents can't carry Jamie and the wheelchair up the stairs."

"Then let's meet in the gym," said one of the junior artists. Apparently she was willing to walk away from her weeks of planning and work in the high school room to accommodate Jamie.

"Well, we've talked about that. I've considered asking to switch classrooms with someone else, too. But Jamie's looked forward to the high school room as much as any of you."

Don heard a few sighs. He watched some students fall deep into thought. Others were making eye contact with each other. He was about to gently chide Mark for whispering to a friend when Mark looked at him and spoke.

"Then Dad, let us carry Jamie up the stairs."

"Really?"

"C'mon. Two of us carry Jamie in a fireman's cradle, two or three of us handle the chair. Unless there's a blizzard or something, we'd have the numbers."

"Yeah." It was Craig, a defensive lineman who was already looking at scholarship letters from Division I schools the summer before his final high school season. "We can cover that. Jamie gets the room; we get Jamie. I like it!"

"Okay, guys. One more thing: If we start this, we have to follow through. When Craig graduates next year, someone else has to step in for him. If Mark's out of town some Sunday, you have to pitch in and do what you can. This is a four-year deal. Can we do it?"

Some responded "Yeah!" like they were in a pre-game locker room. Others nodded and made eye contact with Don. But not one of them refused the challenge.

He called Stan and Ellen from the phone in the church kitchen with the news.

That had been three years and ten months before. Two hundred Sundays—and the kids had never once failed in their mission to Jamie. Don had taken them through their curriculum. The kids caught on to most of it. But Don took a special joy in the commitment they'd shown to Jamie and to each other by following through Sunday after Sunday. For a couple of years, Jamie kept firing zingers to keep class discussions hot before the disease began to reduce his contributions. These days, Jamie would get out a "Jesus . . . rules!" at the end of class and not much else.

Don was waiting for his class this Sunday as was his custom. Mark helped carry Jamie to lead the high schoolers up the stairs, as had become his custom. This Sunday, Mark and Jamie joined their senior classmates in graduation caps and school colors. They'd been honored in the church service before class.

There was the usual bantering in the moments before class began. Then everyone was surprised by a knock at the room's doorway.

"Stan! Ellen! Come join us!" Don and a few of the students scrambled to find places for Jamie's parents.

"Coach, is it okay that we brought treats?" Stan reached into a cooler for sodas. Ellen produced three dozen cupcakes from a container she was carrying.

"No problem here." The kids passed the sodas and cupcakes around, and the banter level rose again.

"We brought these for a reason. We're celebrating the seniors' graduation, and Jamie's graduation into the young adults class." Ellen smiled. "You know, the class that meets on the main level?"

"Jamie's got something to say to you all now." Stan wheeled Jamie into position so he could make eye contact with everyone in the room.

"Guys . . ." Jamie had to catch his breath as he looked from student to student—each one—and managed a small smile. "Coach . . ." The voice was weak, but the eyes still shone. Don smiled back and nodded for Jamie to continue.

"All . . . you . . . thanks!"

One by one, the students got up, walked over to Jamie, and hugged him. When the last one walked away, Jamie rolled his head as if to build up steam and crackled, "Jesus . . . rules!"

No doubt. Don was praying silently in thanks. *Now what do we do for an encore this fall, God?*

Recognizing a Faith Kid

It may sound like Don's kids were "super-Christians." Not really. They were just "faith kids."

We opened the chapter with a working definition of "faith kids." Let's revisit that quickly.

A "faith kid" is a person of any age who responds to a faith relationship with God through Jesus Christ—and continues to grow in that relationship. In other words, "faith kids" are people who somehow show Jesus is alive and well in their hearts, minds, and actions—no matter what their age, no matter where they are in life.

If we break down that definition, we find out that:

1) *Faith kids come in all sizes and ages.* The "kid" part of a faith kid often focuses on pre-adult ages, even in this book. But the basic reference to "kids" here is a simple reminder that all of us who've responded to a faith relationship with God are God's children—even at 30, 60, or 80 years old—even if we're Sunday school teachers! So a faith kid can be anybody. Think about it: Every person mentioned by name in this chapter's story was a faith kid.

2) *Faith kids are people under development.* Don't look for perfection when you're looking for a "faith kid." Look for someone learning and applying their faith week by week.

3) *Faith kids act their ages—for better or worse.* Sorry. Middle-school-aged "faith kids" won't act like miniature adults. But we do expect them to be more mature than upper elementary students. (And, if they're "faith kids," they'll want to grow and mature in response to what they know about God anyway.)

4) *Faith kids are building toward, have established, or are building on a personal relationship with Jesus Christ.* A faith kid may not have prayed the prayer of salvation just yet, but she is building a foundation toward that end through learning and applying God's Word to her everyday life. Faith kids who have that relationship with Jesus are learning to live in response to that relationship—perhaps by doing something as simple as asking "What does God want me to do?" as part of their daily decision making.

5) *Faith kids demonstrate spiritual growth.* Of course, this doesn't mean they'll all demonstrate it in your class simultaneously. That being said, you should be able to see progress in their actions and attitudes based on the impact of God's Word in their lives.

6) *Faith kids live their faith inside and outside the church walls.* This means you won't be the only source of input toward their spiritual growth. There's an element of their development that takes place in your classroom, and an element of their development that can only happen at home.

These six points lead to a seventh:

7) *Faith kids need the kind of spiritual guidance that helps them put their faith into action in everyday life.* In all honesty, this requires appropriate spiritual input from both the church and the home— both Faith Teaching and Faith Parenting. Even though this book's emphasis is on Faith Teaching, you'll discover in the following pages that both church and home play crucial—and distinct— roles in the process of spiritual development.

Think about it: You know some faith kids already, don't you? They just might be the ones looking at you every Sunday morning as you break open that week's lesson to teach. That means you're in a prime position to help "grow" them to the next stage of maturity in faith.

How can you have the greatest impact? By consciously, intentionally fulfilling your part of the church/home link, teamed with your students' families. It's easier than you think.

For Review and Discussion

1. Think about your class for a moment. Who among your students best qualify as faith kids? Why?

2. As best you can tell, which families represented in your class do the best job of nurturing faith kids? What specific things let you know that?

3. Which aspect of being a faith kid (as defined above) would you most like to improve in yourself?

How Does the Church/Home Link Work? 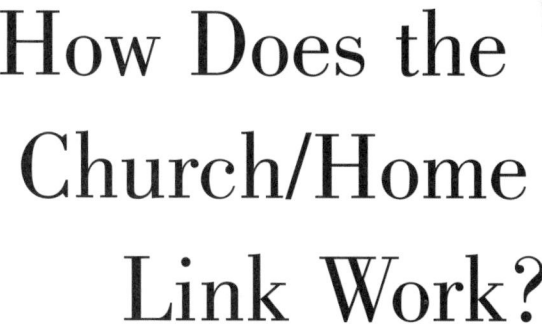2

THE ROLES OF TEACHER AND PARENT in the church/home link are complementary, not identical. Teachers in Sunday school usually work in a more structured teaching setting to help students acquire meaningful Bible content and to encourage them to apply that truth to everyday life. In a less structured setting, parents illustrate values in words and deeds and help children relate God's truth to life, sometimes in "set-aside" time—but more often in more spontaneous situations.

Remember: You're the Sunday school teacher. You don't have to be a parent to your students—unless your kids are in your class!

The parent is your indispensable partner in the church/home link.

Faith Teaching

Dana's schedule caught her coming and going.

Between the carpools, church activities, tutoring, part-time job, and being a wife and mom, she hardly had time to think about her role as a Sunday school teacher—much less plan for it.

But plan for it she did—faithfully, weekly, right on schedule. With craft supplies and class materials in place, Dana was ready to hit her mark every Sunday. She handed out the take-home weeklies like clockwork. She made it a point to connect with each parent at least every other week. Her informal chats with the parents summed up what the kids had studied that Sunday, and why it was so wonderful that their children were in her class.

Dana really believed the kids in her class were wonderful, too. She opened each class session with a "group talk" that allowed her to sense where each of her elementary students was coming from that week. She took in all the information she could from those talks, and followed up where she thought she needed to.

Dana even encouraged the children to bring her their report cards. She lavished praise for their efforts, regardless of the marks. She celebrated each birthday with a cake in class. She took the children for walks, and pointed out the wonders of God's creation in ways they could understand.

"Y'know, Dana, it's almost embarrassing to have Steven in your class." Tracy was Dana's friend, and Steven was her first child. On Tuesday mornings, Tracy and Dana got together for coffee.

"What do you mean?" Dana stirred the whipped cream that topped her hot chocolate.

How Does the Church/Home Link Work?

"There are some weeks I feel like a total slug as a parent when I think about the quality of the hour you spend with Steven at Sunday school. You tell him most of the little things I mean to, and take the walks that I should be making time to take with him. And to be honest, your birthday cake for him made mine look puny.

"How do you do it so well for the kids in your Sunday school class and manage your brood at home?"

The question was probably meant as a compliment. But for some reason, it stung Dana.

"I . . . I don't know. I guess I've never thought about it that way. . . . So how does Jim like his new job?"

Tracy took the verbal bait and ran with it. She was proud of her husband's promotion, so the rest of Tuesday morning at the coffee shop was spent in the details of Jim's office politics.

Dana was grateful for the conversational detour. She was still trying to figure out why the question haunted her. It didn't help when Shannon, her middle schooler, came home that afternoon with a reminder from the family calendar.

"So, Mom, when you're baking cakes for your Sunday school class this week, try to remember that Dad's birthday is coming up on Monday."

Then Dana put Tracy's question from the coffee shop into context. The questions poured through her head a mile a minute.

Am I being so much of a parent in Sunday school that my own family feels neglected?

Do the parents of the kids I teach see me as a help, or competition?
God, where do I draw the line in these roles of teacher and
parent?

What's My Assignment?

Dana has yet to completely resolve those questions. They're not simple ones to answer. That being said, it was revolutionary for her to be confronted with the idea that her efforts in Sunday school might be seen as competition by the parents of her classroom kids. It was also an eye-opener that her own child noticed her profound dedication to Sunday school, and not necessarily in a positive light. Whether Shannon's implication that Dana's Sunday school class took precedence over her family at times is an issue Dana is still working through.

What's my assignment as a Sunday school teacher? Frankly, we would have loved Dana as our elementary Sunday school teacher. But we're not sure how we would respond as Dana's own kids or her spouse, or as parents of children in her class.

One thing we do know: Teaching has a defined role in the church/home link. And sometimes, if we become too much "family" in the teaching role, the bonds in the link suffer.

This isn't to say that we're to become cold, rigid "instructors of the faith." Rather, it's a matter of focusing on our role: Teachers in Sunday school usually work in a more structured teaching setting to help students acquire meaningful Bible content and to encourage them to apply that truth to everyday life.

How Does the Church/Home Link Work?

Let's break this down. If you're teaching, your role is to offer content and help your students come up with a plan to apply that content. What you teach and the order in which you teach it is usually predetermined by the curriculum you use—and that's okay. Because you're probably handling a group over which you have limited control (at least compared to the control most parents could exercise), you need a more structured teaching setting. The group dynamic of a classroom really demands a well-planned lesson. Your goal is to help your students acquire meaningful Bible content and then encourage them to apply that truth to everyday life.

Why is structure so important in your role as a teacher? — Because churches simply don't have the number of staff or volunteers to provide the individualization found in the home. Sunday schools can't organize to meet each student's unique needs, so by necessity they deal in age-appropriate group needs and teaching strategies. On the other hand, the kind of "teachable-moment" Christian education that happens in the home would be a hit-or-miss proposition if it were the only teaching method used in the church. Of course, alert teachers will look for opportunities to build on events that are on students' minds. But they can't rely on that happening every time. They need a plan for teaching, a program for student learning. Otherwise there would be no guarantee that the appropriate Bible content would be learned—and no point of reference to tell whether the church was fulfilling its educational mission.

Make no mistake: Both church and home, both teacher and parent, have their unique roles in God's process of spiritual development. The underlying structure of a curriculum and the church's teachers can enhance and reinforce those roles.

It's a matter of recognizing, valuing, and encouraging the necessary links between church and home. It's a matter of feedback.

Make the Most of Your Feedback Loop

Feedback between the parts of the church/home link is crucial to the strength and health of that link.

The good news is this: It's likely your Sunday school lessons have a built-in feedback loop—all you have to do is use it. Many Sunday school classes follow a simple step-by-step structure, which follows a pattern called "the Natural Learning Cycle":

1) *Need*—The lesson begins by establishing a student's need for more knowledge by capturing a student's interest in the topic. If lessons build on one another (as is often the case in Sunday school curriculum), a review of the previous lesson's main point is part of this step. In this step, the role of the teacher is that of a *motivator.*

2) *Study*—The lesson continues by offering Bible information to the student, and then reviewing it. This is the heart of the lesson. Students can't apply what they don't know, and what we ask them to learn in this step must have significance. (See Chapter 3 for more discussion of this point.) In this step, the role of the teacher is that of an *information giver.*

3) *Application*—This step helps students understand how the Bible content can be applied to everyday life. When students "practice" the Bible lesson in the safety of the classroom, the truth

How Does the Church/Home Link Work?

becomes internalized; it's not just information anymore. This step could involve a game, art project, drama, or many other types of activities. In this step, your role as a teacher is that of a *coach*.

4) *Response*—This step leads the student to commit to one way to put the lesson into practice in the week to come. The teacher's role is that of an *encourager* who invites the students to live what they've learned.

(You can find out more about the Natural Learning Cycle— and get an expanded idea of what your role as a teacher looks like step-by-step through a lesson—in the book *Reach Every One You Teach*, available from Cook Communications Ministries.)

Take a close look at the Natural Learning Cycle as outlined above. There's a built-in connection between church and home. The students "take home" the life application of the lesson content. That's the "feedback" from church to home. And many curriculums will have some kind of debriefing of the week just passed as the lesson opens. That's the "feedback" from home to church. Week by week, the loop continues. The question is, *Are you making the most of it?*

The feedback loop established by sound curriculum can be enhanced in a number of ways:

From church to home:

1) Calls, notes, e-mails and other communications from the teacher to the parents about a student's classroom successes—or challenges

2) Sunday school take-home papers that reflect lesson content

for the week, especially if parents are shown how to use them effectively

3) Invitations for parents to visit or volunteer in the Sunday school class

4) Simple news bulletins to inform parents of curriculum themes and emphases

5) Student crafts that, once taken home, will likely stimulate discussion of lesson content

From home to church:

1) Calls, notes, or other communications from the parents to the teacher about a student's home life, school situations, or special needs

2) Invitations to the teacher to visit the home—or even a short chat after church

3) Asking children questions about take-home papers and crafts to help review and reinforce the lesson.

4) Letting the teacher know about lessons that seemed to have exceptional impact on a student. Few things you can do will be more encouraging!

5) Asking about what subject matter will be covered in the next few weeks. This information could help shape your own family devotional times.

6) Offering to assist in the Sunday school classroom, or to help organize a special event.

How Does the Church/Home Link Work?

We encourage you to add to these lists from your own experience. We especially encourage you to do what you can to put the lists into action.

Your Not-So-Hidden Partner

Remember: The parent is your indispensable partner in the church/home link.

You owe it to your partners, then, to be sensitive to their perspective. If you're a parent as well as a Sunday school teacher, maybe this task isn't so tough. Then again, it can be difficult not to relate to kids primarily as a parent if that's a role you have seven days a week.

Parents are your partners in developing faith kids. But while your focus is Bible content and application through structured lessons, your partners' focus is the transmission of values through everyday life experiences. That doesn't mean that parents won't have structured learning times for their kids—but their structure for learning will be different from the Sunday school lesson.

Take the issue of prayer, for example. Your approach to the topic may involve a story that illustrates the need to pray, Scripture about prayer, opportunities to practice praying, and an encouragement to pray daily throughout the week. A parent's approach, in contrast, may begin with a situation that leads the family to pray together. An alert parent can capitalize on this teachable moment by reminding the child of a Scripture verse that talks about praying in this situation, and then follow that teaching time by actually praying with a child. The parent can afford a more individualized strategy.

The parent can also build on this experience by leading the family in an intentional, focused learning time on prayer, while the experience is still fresh in everyone's mind.

How does the feedback loop work in this case? In most curriculums, prayer is a basic Bible topic that is covered many times at multiple age levels. More than likely, your teaching will have already provided the student a framework of principles and Scriptures on prayer. These prayer principles are honed at home, and then brought back to the classroom for additional structured learning, which are then tested on the home front again—and on, and on.

One more time: The roles of teacher and parent in the church/home link are complementary, not identical. We believe God established it that way. This link is inherent, not imposed.

It isn't difficult to understand, either. If you consider the chart on the next page, you'll see how the two parts of the church/home link are intended to balance one another.

As a Faith Teacher, the church/home link is where you live. The link from church to home begins in your classroom when you encourage your students to live out the Bible truth from your lesson in their homes. It "cycles" the next week, when you ask your students about their success in living out the lesson during the week.

The link from home to church actually begins in the concrete experiences of people with their families. Some of those experi-

CHURCH	HOME
Goal: Development of faith kids	Goal: Development of faith kids
Systematic plan of Bible content to be taught (what educators call a "scope and sequence"); scheduled time and place	Spontaneous, opportunistic, "teachable moments"; topics for intentional teaching times are often a response to family experiences
Foundational principles; application appropriate to most students of particular age level	Personal application, growing out of specific situations
Structured, planned, organized, scheduled	Flexible, fluid, casual, informal, as needed
Targeted to age-level groups	Targeted to individuals
Shaped by the church's Christian education goals	Guided by individual needs
Focuses on things that students of the same age have in common	Focuses on personal uniquenesses
General, universal truths	Contextualized, personalized truths
Needs common to a group	Needs unique to an individual
Help students plan for application	Help students actualize application

ences may be directly related to what went on in your class on Sunday, but many are not. This is the realm of gradual, spontaneous spiritual development. As your students share those experiences with others in the class, they help other students with the crucial task of relating Bible truth to everyday life.

At the bottom line, we believe the link between church and home is as natural—and as necessary—as breathing. There's no need to blur the differences between church and home. You don't have to be the parent, and the parent doesn't have to become the Sunday school teacher. In fact, the church must be the church, and the home the home. Trying to impose superficial similarities between the two won't strengthen the link. Each ministry realm must perform its unique role.

We're not saying your link is perfect. Ours have never been. Still, we know from experience that you, the Sunday school teacher, and your partner, the parent, already have the resources to make the church/home link work as God intended.

And in the chapters to come, you'll find ways to make it work even better.

For Review and Discussion

1. Do you ever feel concerned that you might be stepping on parental "territory" as you teach Sunday school? Why or why not?

2. How do you presently engage the parents or families of your Sunday school students to be your partners in the church/home link?

3. How might you improve the "feedback loop" between your class and the homes of your Sunday school students? What can you do this week to make it better?

The Principle of Content

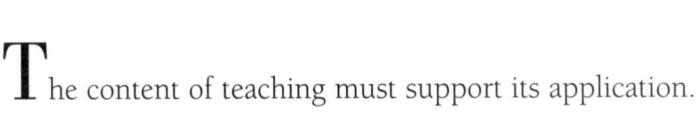

The content of teaching must support its application.

"It's official. I've completely forgotten what it was like to be 13."

Molly looked up from the park bench to watch her own 10-year-old daughter Callie push a neighbor child on the swings. "And there she is, on the doorstep of adolescence."

"'Scuse me, dear. What event produced these comments at this time?" Greg had learned in 15 years of marriage that a significant statement would follow an "It's official" from his wife.

"Sunday school. The girls, especially. I don't remember seventh grade the way they're living it out."

"Count yourself blessed. I don't remember seventh grade at all."

"Gregory!"

Uh-oh. It was the "given name" treatment. Greg knew it was time to cut his losses and give his full attention to Molly. "Okay, so things are different these days. What can you do about it?"

"Well, honestly, I wonder whether the kids in my class have any idea that what I'm trying to teach in Sunday school actually has a real-life application. Especially Brianna. She really has no Christian background—it's kind of a tough home life for her. I just don't think I'm getting the point across; I don't think she understands that she can take what she learns home and do something with it. And if anyone in my class needs to do something positive with it, I think it's Brianna."

Greg was a software analyst by profession. He couldn't help putting his problem-solving skills to work. "Well, let's pick apart this morning's session. Do you usually have a section in the lesson where you suggest some practical application?"

Molly nodded. "Yes, it's there. The problem is, we don't always get to it. We get so wrapped up talking about the Bible content most of the time that the parts of the lesson that follow it get shortchanged."

"You know," Greg observed, "the Bible content is probably intriguing to the kids who have Bible exposure. But the kids without that background may feel kind of lost without some handle on how to apply the Bible away from Sunday school. So if you're really concerned about Brianna . . ."

"I know. Get to the application and make it clear."

The Principle of Content

"You took the words right from my mouth." Greg smiled. "You realize on the open market this consultation would have cost you big bucks, but I'll settle for your triple-cheese lasagna tomorrow night."

"Fine. Just remind me to watch my time in Sunday school next week, Mr. Consultant, sir."

But Greg didn't have to. Molly read and reread the lesson on Saturday to make sure she could summarize each section and keep the discussion moving. She even estimated the time it would take to do each step, and printed the starting time for each step in the margin of her teacher's guide. By Sunday morning she was determined to complete her mission—and the lesson—so Brianna would get a clear picture that the Bible could apply to life at home. The Bible content was simple enough. Basically, it boiled down to "God loves us, so we should show love to others." The memory verse was John 15:12: "My command is this: Love each other as I have loved you."

Molly kept pretty close to her schedule. With a sense of satisfaction and anticipation, she asked the question that opened the application part of the lesson: "So how can we show that we love each other?"

Brianna made a face. "I don't think we need to get mushy in church, do we?"

After everyone had a good chuckle, Molly pressed on. "I want you to divide up in pairs, maybe threes. Figure out a skit or pantomime of one minute or less that shows how we can show we love each other at home, at school, or even here at church."

The kids all took their turns. One school sketch showed kids not letting gossip about a friend go by unchallenged. Another simply showed one student dropping a pile of books, and another helping her pick them up. A sketch about the home front showed a student struggling with keeping a good attitude while obeying his parents—with the good attitude winning out, of course. Brianna and her partner did a great pantomime of a young person helping a senior citizen make her way up the church steps.

Molly then led a brainstorming session. The kids came up with great ideas on how they could show God's love to someone else that week. Molly challenged the students to think of a practical way they could show God's love to someone else this week: "Not out of guilt, not so other people will love us, but just because God showed His love to us." The class closed in a circle prayer.

While the other students hurried out the door, Brianna stayed behind. With a quizzical look, she shrugged and came up to Molly. "You know, I can *do* this stuff, can't I?"

"Sure you can. The Bible won't make much sense until you see that it can work every day, right?"

The Principle of Content

"Wow. Okay, then, I know what I can do this week!" Brianna shouted as she ran out the door.

"Hey, let me know how things turn out for you next week!" Molly called after her.

"No problem!" Brianna's voice came from down the hall.

I hope the other classes were through! Oh, God, whatever Brianna has in mind, please let it work for her. Somehow, please let her see that the Bible can apply every day.

Molly thought of Brianna now and then during the week, and prayed for her. Brianna seemed to have something definite in mind when she left the classroom, and it was all Molly could do to keep from calling her to find out what she was trying to put into action.

On Sunday, Molly opened class with a time to share how the kids had done showing God's love to someone that week. But Brianna didn't come to class in a talkative mood that day. Molly listened to the other students' feedback on the week. She turned her head toward Brianna.

"Oh, me?" Brianna seemed surprised that Molly wanted her to talk.

"Yes, please. Brianna, what did you try this week? How did it work out for you?"

"You know, it was the wildest thing. My aunt lives with us. She works these really weird hours. This week I kept the noise down for Jesus' sake. By Friday, she was hugging me when I came home from school, nearly crying just because I tried to be quiet.

Go figure! So how did I do?"

"Just fine, Brianna. Just fine. Wait'll you see what God wants us to try out this week. . . ."

Watch This Principle

For review here, let's repeat the principle: *The content of teaching must support its application.*

That means what you teach needs to be put into action for the lesson to take root in a student's life.

How do you think Brianna's unchurched family felt when they discovered her changed behavior was due to her putting a Sunday school lesson into action? For starters, it mellowed their feelings about church. Brianna was encouraged when she saw that the application brought results. She received more reinforcement when she reported the results in class the following Sunday. Because the Bible content led directly to meaningful application, the lesson was effective.

At this point we'd like to say something in defense of "content." To some Christian educators, "content" seems to be a dirty word. They conjure up images of stern-faced teachers drilling useless information into bored students. The solution? Downplay content and make Sunday school a time for entertainment, diversion, and fun instead. Don't even call it Sunday *school*—make it sound like fun (because learning is boring). They're satisfied to sneak in a grain or two of Bible information while kids are paying attention to something else. This is Christian education?

The Principle of Content

Our experience has been quite different. We've found that the antidote to boredom is not diversion, but significant content. Now don't get us wrong: we're in favor of fun. We think it's a shame when God's Word is presented as dry, dull, dead data. But we know that few churches can keep kids coming back with entertainment alone. So why would kids decide to come to church instead of hanging out at the mall or playing video games? There's no good reason—unless what they get at church is worthwhile. Here they can meet with other Christians for support and encouragement. Here they can learn—yes, learn!—important things about God and about themselves. Here they can see how God makes a difference in their lives.

So to summarize, teaching significant content and applying it meaningfully to students' lives is one of the best ways to reinforce the church/home link. How can you make this principle work for you?

1) Don't compromise on content. If your primary goal is diversion, you'll be diverted from your Faith Teaching mission. So make sure your curriculum unapologetically communicates significant Bible content geared to the age level you're teaching.

2) Make sure that you don't get so caught up in transmitting information—important as that is—that you never get around to helping students work through how the content can be applied. (Molly's situation in class at the beginning of this story is pretty common.) Use the clock wisely.

3) Make sure your curriculum builds application right into the lesson and encourages students to personalize that application.

There's another important way to use the principle: Let your students know how you're applying the lesson content to your own life. In an appropriate way, when it fits naturally into the lesson, without turning it into a bragging or confession time, let your students hear about how you're doing with that lesson's Bible content. Tell them about the successes and the failures. It's important that you model the fact that being a faith kid is a lifelong calling. We never stop learning and growing—and they need to see that that's normal.

The Principle of Context

4

CHRISTIAN EDUCATION STRATEGIES—at church and home—must address the fullest context of the student's life. Therefore, what happens in the church and what happens in the home must complement each other.

Every year, Naomi's fourth and fifth grade class spent the first few minutes of the Sunday after Thanksgiving putting up Christmas decorations. They strung popcorn. They pinned ornaments to the bulletin board. They made their own decorations to take home.

Usually the kids really enjoyed the break from routine. That's why Naomi noticed Kellie. She just wasn't "into" decorating for some reason.

"Kellie, are you feeling all right?"

"Oh, sure, Mrs. Delehant. It's just—aww, you know—they're not letting us do anything like this at school this year. Christmas must really bug some people!"

Naomi almost launched into a "good old days" retrospective and an analysis on the degeneration of family values in society. Thankfully, she thought better of it.

"Well, Kellie, they can control some things about Christmas—but not everything."

Naomi called the class into session. The day's theme: Witnessing. The theme verse was Acts 1:8: "You will receive power when the Holy Spirit comes on you; and you will be my witnesses in Jerusalem, and in all Judea and Samaria, and to the ends of the earth."

Before long, they were reading the story of a boy who put a sign up in his bedroom window as a public witness of his faith in Jesus. After a while, cars actually slowed down to see what the sign had to say.

Kellie was deep in thought at the end of the story. "So we make Christmas decorations every year . . . why can't I make a sign?"

Naomi nodded. "That's one way you could be a witness this Christmas. Check it out with your parents. I think it's a great idea, Kellie!"

Two weeks later, Naomi was reading the Sunday paper at the breakfast table when she noticed Kellie's picture on the front page of the Lifestyle section! The headline read, "Fifth Grader Reminds Neighborhood of 'The Reason for the Season.' "

And there was Kellie's sign, lettered neatly in her own hand: "Hey, World! It's Jesus' Birthday!!!"

Kellie was beaming when she walked into class that morning. "Mrs. Delehant, did you see the paper today?"

"I sure did, Kellie! Wow, what a witness!"

"It's so cool, Mrs. Delehant! I went home from Sunday school a couple of weeks ago and talked to my parents just like you said. Dad said, 'Make the sign, honey, and we'll see what we can do with it.' Then Mom took me out to get this huge piece of poster board and markers and stuff to laminate the sign. Then I figured out what to put on the sign. It took three days to finish. When I was done with it, Mom laminated it, Dad mounted it on plywood, and we put it on our front lawn with lights around it!"

The other kids started coming into class. They'd seen the paper too.

"Hey, Kellie, cool sign!"

"Mom and Dad said we're driving by your house tonight to see the sign when the lights are on."

"Kellie, what did you use to make the sign with? I think my

parents will let me make one like it too."

Kellie's dad walked in on his way to his own Sunday school class. "Say, Naomi, thanks for the idea. I think you made Kellie's Christmas this year."

"It was really Kellie's idea. I just encouraged her. Looks like Kellie's making Christmas for a lot of other people too. Thanks for letting her follow through with it."

<u>Watch</u> <u>This</u> <u>Principle</u>

Here's the principle of context again: *Christian education strategies—at church and home—must address the fullest context of the student's life. Therefore, what happens in the church and home must complement each other.*

To understand your students' context, keep in mind the places they go during the week. For most school-age children engaged in Sunday school, the three key places that make up their contexts are home, school, and church.

Is it any wonder, then, that school is another "primary proving ground" for Sunday school lesson application?

Kellie's concern for Christmas being "left out" of her public school drove her to take exceptional action. Naomi used a story in the Sunday school lesson to provide an example for her action (although she might not have believed at first that any of her students would follow the lead of the boy in the story). Kellie's parents gave her practical and strategic encouragement. They lived out their faith in God and their support of their daughter in the planning, making, and placement of Kellie's Christmas sign.

Kellie's parents and Naomi were aware of Kellie's distress about the "lack of Christmas" at her school. Naomi's encouragement for Kellie to listen to the lesson was, in part, one way of extending the lesson application to deal with Kellie's response to her school. In that way, Naomi was dealing with Kellie's broader life context. Kellie's parents, in modeling and encouraging faith-building behavior in their daughter, did the same.

So how do you make the principle of context work better in the church/home link?

1) Pay close attention to what your students are saying verbally and nonverbally throughout class. Remember, one rightly-timed question (like Naomi's question to Kellie about how she was feeling) could give you substantial clues about a student's broader life context, and ideas on how to help.

2) Keep reminding yourself and your students that what they learn needs to be applied at home, at school, and at church. That will reinforce in your students the idea that you understand the context they face beyond the Sunday school classroom.

3) Look for ways to keep in touch with your students' parents. Find what works for you—occasional notes, phone calls, conversations at church, whatever. (One teacher has a practical tip: If you're teaching older kids and decide to write to the kids or the parents or both, consider using postcards. It's a natural human tendency to wonder about what the teacher is writing, so make it

easy to snoop! You'll find that parents and kids will trust you more if they know you have nothing to hide.) Express interest in how things are going at school, and assure them that you're praying for them.

It might help your students if they understand more of your own life context beyond the Sunday school classroom too. Let them know where you work, what your hobbies are, and something about your family. You'll set the example for the kids you teach to talk more easily about their everyday lives—and your class sessions will be the richer for it.

The Principle of Focus

T HE FOCUS OF A SUNDAY SCHOOL LESSON is the impact of God's Word on groups of individuals; the target for content is the common ground shared by students at a certain developmental stage. The focus of a home lesson is the impact of God's Word on an individual; the target for content is what uniquely suits one person.

When both church and home keep their focus, students can focus too.

Jeff and Josh were the live wires of Tom's elementary Sunday school class. There was no doubt about that.

But even though they were identical twins, Tom had noticed Jeff and Josh didn't always pick up on the same things.

Take last Sunday. It was an introduction to the idea that the Church is the Body of Christ. The theme verse was 1 Corinthians 12:27: "Now you are the body of Christ, and each one of you is a part of it."

It takes a while for metaphors to sink in with children, and last Sunday was no exception. But after a while, most of the class was catching on.

"I can be a hand, and help other people."

"I can be an ear, and listen to good things."

"I want to be an eye, and watch out for what other people need."

Tom was impressed with his class. They basically caught on to the idea that the people of the church make up the Body of Christ. Not a bad morning's work, Tom was thinking to himself.

That was when Josh piped up. "Teacher?"

"Yes, Josh."

"How can a church be a body?"

"Well, the people who are the church make up the Body of Christ. That's what I mean."

"But what about the church?"

"The people?"

"No. You know, the church."

"Like the building?"

"Yeah. That's it. The building."

"What about the building?"

"How can the building be a body?"

Flashes of the Abbott and Costello "Who's On First?" routine played in Tom's mind. Worse, he was losing the rest of the class.

"Josh, I'll tell you what. You talk this over with your parents and Jeff this week. If you still have questions by next Sunday, we'll talk it over again then. Deal?"

"Deal, Teacher."

Tom made it a point to catch Jerry and Judy—the parents of the twins—right after church. "I think today's Sunday school lesson confused Josh a bit. The class time really didn't allow for his questions. Do you think you could talk some with him about the difference between the church as a building and the church as people?"

"No problem. How did Jeff seem to do with the idea, by the way?" Jerry smirked as though he anticipated the answer.

"You know, Jeff seemed to catch on pretty quickly today."

Judy giggled. "We've found out that the boys may look alike, but that they sure don't handle information the same way."

Jerry nodded. "Jeff's our 'idea boy.' Josh can tackle anything that's active or practical. But the crossover between them has yet to develop. So let me get this straight: We need to explain the difference between the church as a building and the church as people, right?"

"That's about the size of it. If it's still a problem by next Sunday, I'll spend some more time with Josh and try to explain it again. Thanks."

"Hey, we're in this together. Thanks for letting us know."

The family made their way to their traditional fast food drive-through. Kids' meals in hand, they drove to a park not far from their home and found an empty picnic table. After a quick round of "Rock, Paper, Scissors," Josh won the privilege of saying grace. Judy passed out the food and the ketchup for fries. Following tradition, Jerry took the kids' meals toys and put them in his pocket until the boys had finished their lunches. Then with a deep breath, Jerry pursued the conversation.

"So, guys, what did you learn in Sunday school today?"

Jeff shrugged the "no big deal" shrug. "We learned that the church is the Body of Christ."

Josh frowned. "Yeah, and I don't get it."

"What part don't you get?" Jerry needed to find some point he could clarify.

Josh thought for a minute. "All of it."

"Like what, son?"

"I don't see how a building can become a body. Especially Jesus' body."

"You know something, Josh? I don't either. See, the 'church' that is talked about in the Bible means 'people'—not a building."

Josh furrowed his brow. "So how do people become one body? They're a bunch of different bodies!"

Judy joined in. "But when people work together and do all the things that Jesus wants us to, it's like we become one body working together."

"So why do we call the building the church?"

"That's a good question, buddy. All I can figure is that the people who are the church spend so much time in the building that we end up calling the building 'the church.' Maybe we shouldn't, but we do."

Jeff nodded toward his brother. "So, do you get it now?"

Josh worked his tongue in his mouth a few seconds. "I think so. The church isn't a building. It's a bunch of people who love Jesus!"

Jerry called Tom with the good news that afternoon.

Watch This Principle

The principle of focus is crucial to successful Christian education. It's just as important to the church/home link too. Let's review: *The focus of a <u>Sunday school lesson</u> is the impact of God's Word on groups of individuals; the target for content is the common ground shared by students at a certain developmental stage. The focus of a <u>home lesson</u> is the impact of God's Word on an individual; the target for content is what uniquely suits one person.*

That's the principle of focus. Now, here's the payoff: When both church and home keep their focus, students can focus too.

Did you ever feel overwhelmed as a student? Maybe it was in high school calculus or trigonometry. (At least those were the classes that overwhelmed us.) You walked in, sat down, looked at the book, realized you didn't understand it, listened to everyone else in the room talk, and realized you didn't understand them either—and then you panicked.

If you had a good teacher, you were encouraged to stick around. Maybe you'd learn something in the class sessions just by being there. If you had a really good teacher, you found yourself in one-on-one sessions with someone who knew the subject and could answer the questions that just couldn't be covered in class.

Some of your students feel that same panic about content you cover in Sunday school. It isn't that they're woefully behind the other students' development. In fact, you'll likely discover that the students switch places in the "panicked student seat" from time to time.

If you know of such a student, now's the time to call for one-on-one help—on the home front.

Your focus in Sunday school, rightly, is a class session based on group needs. That doesn't mean you ignore individuals; in fact, a well-developed lesson can make sure that every student feels successful in at least part of the lesson. But due to your limited time, it does mean that some of their unique questions have to be addressed outside of class.

Your built-in partner here is the parent. Hopefully, the parent shares your concern for your student's spiritual development. (We understand that this is not always the case, but hang in there with us.)

The parent can take the time, as Jerry and Judy did for Josh, to clarify a student's unique questions. The parent rightly holds the position of one-on-one spiritual tutor for the child you teach. The parent should connect with the child in a manner that is more individualized. It wouldn't usually be expedient for you as a Sunday school teacher to try to connect individually with each student regarding lesson content. Likewise, it wouldn't be right for a parent to use a formally structured group lesson in an "up close and personal" session with a child.

Here are a few hints for bringing the principle of focus to your Faith Teaching:

1) Remember your role is to teach a group of students. You should recognize their individuality in the teaching process, but because of the limitations of the teaching situation your content and delivery will be primarily focused on group learning.

2) If you sense a child needs more individual attention in discussing an issue that wasn't resolved in your class, let the parents know about the issue and ask for their help in resolving the question at home.

3) If a child really isn't receiving spiritual support at home, you may need to offer appropriate one-on-one time to help him resolve his unique questions—but that time probably shouldn't be taken from the rest of your students. Encourage the child to stay a few moments after class or to come a few moments early the next Sunday to discuss his questions.

If both the church and the home actively engage their proper focuses as partners in spiritual development, the potential for faith kid development is staggering. (And, the relationship is a great illustration of how people work together as the Body of Christ, the Church . . . which, as Josh would now tell us, is not a building, but a bunch of people who love Jesus.)

The Principle of Location

6

LOCATION—CHURCH OR HOME—HELPS DETERMINE the most effective approach for Christian education strategy.

Susan wanted to hear those golden words one more time.

"Becky, will you repeat that? I want to make sure I heard you clearly."

"Susan, Jack and I want to follow up what you're doing with Brandon in Sunday school. We want a copy of your lesson book, or something like that, to help us reinforce what you're teaching him."

"Wow! I can't believe this!"

"Oh, I'm sorry . . . Is it wrong for me to ask?"

"No, no, not at all! I think I'm in the middle of every Sunday school teacher's dream, that's all! I've never had a parent ask this before. It's wonderful!"

"Other parents aren't using Sunday school lessons at home? Then what do they do for family devotions?"

Susan was about to laugh out loud. Then she noticed that Becky was completely serious. That's when Susan shifted the course of the conversation.

"Becky, can I ask you a few questions?"

"Sure."

"What do you think people do for family devotions?"

"I'd imagine they pray. Probably they'd have some Bible reading. I think it would really help the kids to have something structured just for them, though. That's why I thought I'd start with Brandon's Sunday school lessons. They'd fit his age and interest, and he'd be hearing the same thing all week."

"Becky, what did your family do for devotions when you were growing up?"

Becky gave a slight shrug and looked at the floor. "We didn't have any. I had no idea that a home could be Christian until a few years ago when Jack and I tried this church out on a Christmas Eve. We kept coming back. We both asked Jesus into our hearts not long after that. We really want to do the right thing for Brandon.

"But neither of us have real family experience to know what devotions with Brandon should look like. We just know we need to start somewhere, so I figured maybe the stuff you're learning in Sunday school might work."

"Well, it might. But you'd have to revise it a lot to have it work at home like it does here. You see, they write Sunday school lessons for groups of students. They also tend to write them for structured time—maybe more structured than you'd like to be at home. Could I make a suggestion?"

"Please!"

"I don't want you to give up on following through with the Sunday school lesson. Brandon should come home with an idea of something he'll put into action based on that week's lesson. If you'd ask him to tell you what that is right after church each Sunday, and then encourage him to follow through, that would really help.

"Brandon also brings a take-home paper with him each week. That paper usually has a story or two, some ideas for Bible reading through the week, and even activities that will either reinforce what he heard that Sunday or set him up for the next Sunday's lesson. If you want a tie-in with Sunday school, that's probably your best resource."

"That's the story paper with the colored picture on the front?"

"That's right."

"You know, every once in a while Jack or I will read a story through with Brandon in that paper, but we haven't looked at much else in it."

"Don't feel bad about that. I don't look at Jesse's take-home paper every week, and, as a Sunday school teacher, I should know better!"

"You're sure that's better than your lesson book?"

Susan nodded. "Absolutely. Because my lesson book is designed for groups, a lot of the activities just won't translate to the individual sessions you could have with Brandon at home. It's great for teaching general principles. But Brandon probably needs a different kind of resource for the home environment.

"See, at home you can really dig into individual questions Brandon has that might never get answered here. You can take whatever time you need, or keep your session really short, or take advantage of some on-the-spot situations that you think would teach Brandon something important about God.

"Maybe it would help for you to think about it like this: At Sunday school we learn what God's Word says and try to give Brandon an example or two of how to apply it every day. I encourage every student, including Brandon, to make a plan for applying the Bible truth. That application has to be done outside the class, when the kids are at home or at school. Because you're right there during his week, you can encourage him to follow through on his plan. But you do a whole lot more, too. You don't have to be limited to the subject of last Sunday's lesson. You can start with any number of life situations and show Brandon how God's Word applies to them.

"The kind of spiritual teaching you do really depends upon where you are. You'll do something different after dinner than you will spur-of-the-moment when there's a lesson to be taught. I do something entirely different in Sunday school than I do at home. My kids need something a lot less structured than what usually happens in a classroom.

The Principle of Location

"For example, each day we use devotions from devotional books written especially for children, either at breakfast or after the evening meal. There are a bunch of good books available for that."

"Can you show me where to find them?"

"Sure." Susan was beginning to realize how much she'd assumed about Becky's knowledge of Christian books and resources. Susan was aware of them largely because she'd been raised in the church; she loved browsing at Christian bookstores. Becky had never been exposed to what was available in Christian publications—and it only made sense. Why would she have been?

"Becky, one more thing. We do a special family night every Thursday. There's a whole line of books that explain how to put that whole night of activity together. The nights are a lot of fun, and the activities are just right for the family. They're not designed to be like Sunday school at all. The Bible lesson and prayer are still there, but the time is more personal than we could ever be here in class.

"Tell you what, Becky. Are you free Tuesday for lunch?"

"Yes, I'm free the whole day."

"Can you meet me at the mall around 11:30? There's a Christian bookstore there that has all this kind of material. I can show you examples of everything we've talked about. I'd be happy to chat with you about what might work for you, Jack, and Brandon at home. Everything you do there can only help me at Sunday school."

Watch This Principle

The principle of location is really pretty simple: *Location—church or home—helps determine the most effective approach for Christian education strategy.*

One of the most valuable lessons from Susan's example is that she recognized the need to alter her teaching strategy according to where she was. She was the first to point out that what worked at Sunday school wouldn't be as effective at home—because the situations at church and home are distinctly different.

Sunday school has to focus on group learning. Home lessons can focus more on individual questions and needs. Sunday school has to deal with general principles of God's Word. Home lessons can deal with more specific life applications of God's Word. (For a complete table on how Christian education strategies tend to be different, according to home or church location, refer back to page 39.)

Keep this principle simple as you use it to reinforce the church/home link. Don't feel like you ever have to blur the line between the church and home as you teach. God has called you

The Principle of Location

to teach Sunday school. Let those things that make Sunday school so crucial to spiritual development—group learning, transmission of general principles, a systematic and structured approach to God's Word—drive your strategy there. If you're a parent, shift gears to a more personalized and less structured approach for the sake of your children when you're at home. Both kinds of teaching are essential to spiritual development.

Letting each location drive the appropriate Christian education strategy is crucial to the health of the church/home link. Here are some hints to make this principle work to its fullest for you:

1) Keep working the strengths of the Sunday school classroom to your advantage. Everything from peer interaction to greater structure can be a blessing to both you and the students you teach. Recognize, reinforce, and exploit those strengths.

2) Help the parents or families of your students recognize the distinct advantages of Christian education at home that you simply don't have at Sunday school. Many parents feel intimidated by the thought of doing Christian education at home; they may think they need professional training to be effective. You can encourage them by pointing out that their opportunities to use everyday situations to reinforce God's Word far exceed your opportunities to do the same. You may need to remind them that their role as a parent naturally offers inroads to a child's spiritual life that you don't have. And, like Susan, be willing to offer help or suggestions if a parent expresses a need.

3) Be ready to suggest resources that could enhance Christian

education at home. For starters, show parents how to use your students' Sunday take-home papers to their best advantage. Then you might want to point them toward home devotional products that will assist them in their efforts to make God's Word come alive for their kids. (*Faith Parenting*, the partner to this volume, might be a good place to start.)

Don't forget this, either: Just as Susan discovered with Becky, we cannot assume that parents have the same knowledge of Christian education resources for the home as we do. In fact, we are discovering that "first generation" Christian adults who bring their children to Sunday school have a significant learning curve about the resources available to Christians today—including publications, music, and where to get these resources.

For the church/home link to work best, the church must be the church and the home must be the home. Each has a God-ordained role to play in spiritual development. Each must take up its unique role in that process for the successful growth of faith kids.

The Principle of Connectivity

T HE CHURCH AND HOME ARE INHERENTLY CONNECTED by a well-executed "need-content-application-response" lesson at church, its application at home, and the student's return to church for accountability and reinforcement.

Work this feedback loop for all it's worth.

Sometimes the simple investments are the ones that pay back the most.

Caryn made simple investments in her preschool class. She took the extra few minutes during Sunday school to make sure the children understood the lesson theme. She carefully reviewed the "action item" for the week with the kids too.

Faith Teaching

Changed behavior at home was one way parents could see that Sunday school was a benefit to their children—and occasionally the parents needed convincing.

Danny came from one such home. His parents weren't necessarily hostile toward Sunday school. They were just "solidly neutral" about it. They were of the opinion that Sunday school was a take-it-or-leave-it option—and almost half the time, they left it. The time spent in church service was enough for them.

But Caryn wondered if Danny felt the same way. He was so enthusiastic about being in Sunday school. He loved being with the other children. And every time Danny walked in the room on Sunday, he announced his presence with a bold, "Hi, Miss Simms! Guess what? I did what we said I should do the last time I was here!" Every time, Danny would launch into a story about how he did the home response part of the lesson he'd heard the last time he was there. Given that "the last time" might have been two or three weeks before, Danny's memory was pretty remarkable.

One Sunday, Caryn heard that Danny was in the hospital for a tonsillectomy. Again, she made some simple investments. She sent a get-well card to Danny. She called Danny's home to let Danny and his parents, Mike and Shelly, know that Danny's Sunday school class was praying for him.

Shelly had answered the phone. She seemed genuinely moved by Caryn's message on behalf of the class. "And, Miss Simms, . . ."

"Please call me Caryn."

"Caryn, thanks so much for your card. Ever since he received

The Principle of Connectivity

it, he's been sleeping with it under his pillow. You know, four year olds don't get that much mail. Except for the cards from his grandparents, yours is the only one he's received. That made his day."

"I'm glad to do it. Danny's a wonderful asset to have in class. I love to have him there."

The conversation turned to small talk after that. Caryn chatted about how gratifying it was for her to hear Danny tell about what he'd done at home in response to the last Sunday school session he'd attended. Shelly talked about her surprise that Sunday school gave that kind of "homework"—and what a kick both she and Mike got out of Danny "bringing the lesson home."

"You know, that's one of the most encouraging things I can hear as a Sunday school teacher, Shelly. I love hearing it from him, and I love hearing it from you, too. Please call me anytime you have questions about what we're teaching Danny. You're welcome to sit in on a class, too."

"Really?"

"Absolutely. Especially if you're willing to help with crafts!"

"Well, thanks for the invitation!"

Nice enough on the phone. But Caryn had heard enough pleasantries from parents over the years that she kept her enthusiasm in check. Besides, it seemed that she'd connected far better with Shelly than she'd ever dreamed possible.

So it was better than Caryn expected when Danny came into class that Sunday with his parents in tow. "Danny kept sleeping with your get-well card under his pillow all week, right through last night." Mike looked around at the classroom and whistled softly. "Wow, has Sunday school changed since I was here!"

"You know what Danny told us this morning?" Shelly picked up the conversation as though she and Caryn were still connected over the phone. "We gave him the option of coming to Sunday school and church today or not. He's much better, but the doctor said not to push him too hard. 'I have to be in Sunday school,' Danny said. 'They need me there.'"

"Hi, Miss Simms! Guess what? I did what we said I should do the last time I was here!" Danny hadn't missed a beat from losing his tonsils.

"Let's get everyone together so we can hear about it, Danny. I'm so glad you're back! We really need you here."

Shelly and Mike looked out of place for a moment, then they sat down with the children in the circle. "Ready for some help with crafts today, Miss Simms?"

Watch This Principle

Let's review the principle of connectivity: *The church and home are inherently connected by a well-executed "need-content-application-response" lesson at church, its application at home, and the student's return to church for accountability and reinforcement.*

Caryn Simms continues to work this principle to the hilt. You might not expect four year olds to be such prime candidates for a feedback loop, but they are. Part of Caryn's "secret" is that her lesson follows what we call the Natural Learning Cycle (see Chapter 2).

She communicates simply and clearly. Her lesson content is present-ed in easy-to-understand words. She sets up the "response" part of the lesson in a simple activity a four year old can do at home. So her students come back week after week with reports of success—and as the old adage says, "Success breeds success."

Perhaps you could tell from Caryn's story presented here that Caryn is a listener. She loves to listen to her students' successes. She enjoys engaging their parents in conversation. Listening is a crucial part of a successful feedback loop. Please don't underesti-mate its positive benefits in the church/home link.

Caryn applies each part of the feedback loop to her teaching strategy every week. First, she utilizes the "need-content-applica-tion-response" lesson format to her advantage. Second, she takes time to set up the "home response" part of the lesson so her stu-dents will succeed with it. Finally, she takes time at the beginning of each lesson to listen to her students' success stories. It's a sim-ple form of accountability that encourages students to follow through with the home response step.

Here are some hints, then, for your successful application of the connectivity principle:

1) Check your curriculum to see if it follows a basic "need-content-application-response" format. If it does, it already facili-tates the feedback loop that is so crucial to the church/home link. If your lessons aren't structured this way, consider adapting the lessons to include something that your students can apply during the week—and then talk about in the next session.

2) Review and/or revise the "take-home response" from each lesson to ensure that as many of your students as possible will succeed in doing it. This can be a delicate balance, especially for students from the middle elementary years and up. You don't want to make it so simple that it holds no intrigue for your students, but you can't afford to make it impossible, either.

3) Review the response part of the lesson with your students both at the end of the current session and at the beginning of the next one. Your students need to see that you take the lesson truth seriously. Spending time to clarify what the home application will be and to debrief the class for success stories at the beginning of the next session will do just that.

4) If you notice that a student is not taking the lesson application home, contact the student's family and talk about it. Every parent will have his or her own "take" on the importance of home response activities. This call isn't the time to preach about the virtues of Sunday school, but rather a time to get a sense of what the child faces on the home front. As a bonus, you might be surprised at the number of parents who become your allies after these calls.

Believe it or not, most kids who are in your Sunday school class would love it if you nurtured a significant connection with them through the church/home link. They'd come to your class with a feeling like Danny's: "They need me here."

The tools are in your hands already—so make the most of this feedback loop.

The Principle
of Maturation

EACH STUDENT WILL MATURE IN A UNIQUE WAY, not in lock-step with other students.

Maturation involves more than "head knowledge," too. It encompasses every aspect of a person's life development.

"Let me get this straight. You're saying that having a kid changes your life more than getting married?"

Kurt chuckled. "Hands down, Randy. No contest." Kurt got a lot of pleasure in teaching this young marrieds' class. "But don't take my word for it. Let's hear from some of you who have children."

There was no lack of volunteered information.

"It's a different kind of change, and more change."

"More diaper changing too. We had twins!"

"It's really weird. Even cleaning up after your own kid—diapers, spit-up on the suit jacket, baby food on the kitchen floor—isn't so bad. And I have a weak stomach."

"You'll never fall in love with someone so fast in your life."

"That's right. And there's the five-minute rule: You hold your baby for five minutes, and you're ready to die for the little ankle-biter."

Kurt used that to transition into a discussion of Psalm 127:3, a theme verse of the day:

"Sons are a heritage from the LORD,
children a reward from him."

The class session went on. Kurt noticed that Randy had the proverbial "deer-in-the-headlights" look on his face: The inevitable was about to happen, and he was too paralyzed to do anything about it. But Kurt had felt much the same way one week away from JoAnn's first due date too. After class, he made his way to Randy's side. "So, Randy, are you and Keri ready for the big day?"

The Principle of Maturation

Keri answered for her husband. "Well, the bag's been packed for two weeks. Randy has the numbers for the hospital and the doctor preprogrammed into his cell phone. The nursery's been ready for a month, and both of our mothers are ready to hop on a plane when we call to tell them I'm in labor."

"Wow! You two are more ready than I knew how to be!"

Randy still looked unsettled. "I still have this nagging feeling that I'm forgetting something, or about to lose something. I guess I'm not as ready as I'd like to be."

"Really? How so?"

"I don't know exactly. I guess I've heard so much about how much children tie you down that I'm getting scared. I don't know if I'm ready for it."

Keri shook her head. "Randy, you weren't sure you were ready for marriage, either. But once we set the date, you knew it was right, and you were ready in time to say the vows."

"Yeah. But this is—well, think about it. We can't go out at the drop of a hat anymore. We can't 'live off love alone'; the kid will have to eat. That means I have to start thinking about getting promoted, or switching jobs for more money. Then there's school, and tying ourselves to his schedule, and—aww, maybe I will be ready. I just don't feel it yet."

"Randy, give yourself a break. JoAnn and I thought we were really ready for kids. We waited 10 years into our marriage before the first one came along. We'd read every baby book on the shelves, had the poor kid's diet slated out for the first three years of her life, and were still surprised every day of parenthood. You know the Sorensons? They *wanted* to wait five years before having children, and Katy was pregnant within three months of their wedding. They lived as though they weren't having a child for a few months, then did the catch-as-catch-can approach to creating a nursery for their baby. I think they finally finished it when the kid was a teenager. But their little boy turned into a super young man anyway.

"The point is that God will make you into the dad you're supposed to be if you let Him. No two people develop into parents the same way, or in the same kind of timing. When's your due date? Thursday, right? God will have you ready to be the parent of a newborn child by then. You'll mature into the role of a parent for a preschooler, a teenager, and all that, when the time comes. But that's the operative phrase here: when the time comes."

Oddly enough, though most predicted due dates are a little off, Randy and Keri's held. Bryce was born a healthy boy that Thursday. As his Sunday school classmates had told him, Randy was completely smitten with his son. Randy came to Sunday school class early whenever he had new pictures of Bryce to show. He and Keri quickly blended into the other young parents' discussions of where the best bargains for disposable diapers were that week, and when they'd begin putting Bryce on solid food.

Randy had matured into the role of a young father very well, it seemed. One affirmation came to Kurt's attention the next Father's Day. Kurt assigned the fathers in his class to write a Father's Day letter to God. Randy wrote,

The Principle of Maturation

Dear God,

Before I became a father, I hadn't given the gift of Your Son much thought. Now, as a dad myself, I am totally in awe that You, God, would allow Your only Son to die for our precious little boy, my wife, and me.

Thanks for letting me be a father, too.

Randy

<u>Watch</u> <u>This</u> <u>Principle</u>

Here's another look at the principle of maturation: *Each student will mature in a unique way, not in lockstep with other students.*

Teachers of children have, by and large, learned to anticipate this truth. Teachers of adults may bypass this principle in their approach to Christian education, thinking that adults no longer have to deal with issues of maturation.

But of course, they do—and just as much as children. (We'll explore this more fully in Chapter 19.) The point for us to recognize is that each of our students—adult and child alike—matures in a unique way.

Kurt brought this point to bear very well in describing how the Sorensons' process of maturing into parenthood differed from his own. In so doing, he likely comforted Randy with the truth that God brings people to points of maturity in different ways.

That example is not so different from the various ways and times God uses to teach children lessons about personal responsibility. For example, some teenagers still haven't shown much evidence of a work ethic, while some nine year olds are profitable entrepreneurs. That isn't to say that these teens all won't mature into fine adult workers—it's just to say that their points of maturation differ.

This leads to another point of the principle that we teachers have to keep in mind: Maturation involves more than "head knowledge," too. It encompasses every aspect of a person's life development. Sometimes experience is the necessary factor in bringing about maturity in a given area. Marriage and parenthood are two of those areas that come to mind. You can have very biblical ideas about marriage and parenthood before experiencing either one of them—but it's the experiential development that will bring about the maturation of those ideas.

So how can you make the most of the maturation principle in your Faith Teaching role?

1) As much as possible, trust God's timing in bringing appropriate maturation to each of your students. We all understand (from experience) that there are times when we have to call for greater maturity from students. At the same time, we want to encourage realistic expectations according to their stage of development. (Again, you can find out more about those expectations in the age-level section of this book, Chapters 12-19.)

2) Realize—and help your students' families realize—that even students in the same age group will mature at different rates. It's only natural for teachers and parents alike to desire that their students match the perceived maturity of the student in class who seems to be

"more advanced" than the others. The more these comparisons can be avoided (like, "Why can't you be more like Johnny?"), the better.

3) Reassure your students that they're not likely to mature in exactly the same way—or at exactly the same pace—as others. It's easy for us to apply this to the realm of physical growth, but we should be just as ready to apply this principle to the realm of spiritual development too.

4) Patience is a virtue that needs to be put into practice by the teacher, the parent, and the child alike. Watching for maturity in a student is like waiting for water to reach a boil. If you wait and watch second-by-second for the results, you might believe they'll never happen.

Faith kids need to know that God values them just as they are— and also, that He wants them to develop into all they can become. You can help this process by reinforcing the truth that maturity is an issue that God works out on a person-by-person basis.

The Principle
of Humanity

9

T HE GOAL OF CHRISTIAN TEACHING, whether at church or at home, is to put a human voice to God's Word and a human model to God's ways.

Les had heard the story before. This was the first time he'd heard it from Emily, though. It was the kind of story that you never get used to hearing.

"Les, I'm sorry. I just have a real problem relating to God as a loving Father. I mean, you tell me that's what He is, and I want to believe it. But what does a loving father look like? All mine ever did—from the time I was seven until I ran away at sixteen—was use me for whatever he wanted. I just don't have any point of reference."

Les knew part of Emily's story from her own stories around the circle in his single adults Sunday school class. The picture he'd had of her until this day was that of a second-career single mother who had done a remarkable job of "pulling herself up by her own bootstraps." She talked openly about earning a GED in her mid-thirties, then pursuing an associate's degree in accounting, and now a bachelor's degree in education. She'd made her way on her own in the nearly 15 years since her husband had left her. She'd been single-handedly raising their two children during that time, and was looking forward to a fulfilling career as a middle school teacher.

"Emily, I know that took a lot for you to say. Thanks for your honesty. I wish I had a good answer for that question for everyone who's been through what you have—but I don't. All I can do is ask you to stick around with us. Maybe you'll find at least part of the answer you need."

"Fair enough. Thanks for listening."

It was three weeks later when Les noticed the birthday list of the students in his class. Emily's birthday would be the Monday after this week's session. That meant her party would take place over cake and coffee during the transition time between church and Sunday school.

Les asked Jenny Rogers to get Emily to the classroom a few minutes after the other singles could make it there. Three other students coordinated the cake and coffee. Since it was Emily's first birthday as part of the class, the "veteran singles" followed their tradition for "first-timers" and chipped in to buy her a study Bible.

You could have knocked Emily over with a feather when she walked into the classroom with Jenny and everyone started singing "Happy Birthday." She smiled and giggled like a schoolgirl at first. Then she said, "I may cry here. I'm sorry. You know, this is the first birthday party I've had in over 30 years that I didn't pay for myself." She composed herself and cut the cake.

Then she unwrapped the study Bible. She ran her hands over the cover, looked at her name stamped on the front, and raised her head to look around at the class. "I don't know what else to say. You really are like a family here, aren't you?" The impact of her own statement seemed to sink in at that moment. She thanked the group with a series of handshakes and a few hugs before Les called the class to order.

That was a turning point for Emily. In the next few months, she began to refer to her "Heavenly Father." She also began showing His love to others outside the class. She took on the mentoring of a single mother in the church whose circumstances were similar to her own 15 years earlier. Emily attended Lamaze classes with her, held her hand when the baby came, and still lightens her load by helping with child care when she can.

Emily stopped Les after class again not long ago. "Les, I can't tell you how much this class means to me. You were so patient. The others have taken me in like I was one of their own."

"That's because you are, Emily."

"You all have wrapped the human arms of God around me. You've helped me heal. I'll never forget who my Heavenly Father is because of you."

Watch This Principle

It bears repeating: *The goal of Christian teaching, whether at church or at home, is to put a human voice to God's Word and a human model to God's ways.*

"Putting a human voice to God's Word" may seem to be more relevant to the Sunday school teacher. Les is certainly competent in the classroom; that portion of the principle is running "full steam ahead." Still, we can't escape the fact that he and the rest of the singles class worked hard at being the "human model to God's ways" for Emily too.

Birthday parties and gifts may not seem like much, but they just might change the lives of some of your students. This isn't an encouragement for Sunday school to supplant the role of the home in a student's life. But you might need to find out how you can best complement what's going on at home, simply to give Sunday school a human touch for the sake of the student.

Being both the "human voice" of God's Word and the "human model" of God's ways is crucial to your students' spiritual development. If teaching by word alone is all a student experiences in Sunday school, the student may conclude that the Word is either impossible to live out, or completely irrelevant to everyday life. Otherwise, someone would be demonstrating how to live God's

The Principle of Humanity

Word, right? If teaching by model alone is all that happens in Sunday school, the student might conclude that Christianity has no real object of faith—like Jesus Christ—and is only a set of lifestyle principles stated slightly differently than those of, say, scouting.

Having said that, here are a few hints to help you make the most of the humanity principle for the church/home link.

1) Remember that you can be both a human voice for God's Word and a human model of God's ways as you teach Sunday school. Your job is to teach Bible content and help plan application, certainly. But your methods and attitude while you teach can be wonderful tools through which you model God's ways, too.

2) Make it a point to reach out to those students who seem to have a problem understanding or relating to God as a person. They are likely the students who most need to connect a human voice with His Word and a human model to His ways. Students who've just moved to the community need to feel at home. The more welcome and safe they feel in your class, the more they'll be able to open up to the Word of God.

3) Suggest ways that your students can become a human voice for God's Word and a human model for God's ways. Call your students to this challenge as they respond to the lesson at home, perhaps suggesting specific ways they can act on this principle. Emily, for instance, was certainly modeling God's ways by taking on the mentoring of a younger single mother in the church. Your students might be able to take on volunteer teaching roles for the church at times, too, to put a human voice to God's Word. (Both of us were introduced to teaching at church as teen Vacation Bible School volunteers and Sunday school assistants.)

Make no mistake: this principle of humanity is the litmus test that some of your students are using to evaluate your class sessions, and whether they want to continue to be a part of them. It might also be the element by which your parent partners in the church/ home link determine whether their children keep coming to Sunday school. Your authenticity has more power than you know.

Most importantly, this principle reminds us that we could be "the only Jesus" some of our students may ever see or hear. Let's pray that we may become more transparent, so that our lives may point our students to Him.

The Principle of Transfer

10

THE TRANSFER OF A "LEARNED PRINCIPLE" from church to home, or from home to church, cannot be legislated or manipulated—only nurtured.

But do we ever love it when it happens!

If anything on earth proved that God has a sense of humor, it was that both Daniel and Douglas were in Jim's fourth and fifth grade Sunday school class at the same time.

The boys were stairsteps. Daniel was maybe an inch taller than his younger brother, but Douglas had a more stocky build and likely outweighed Daniel by 10 pounds. These were important facts for Jim to remember when the boys came running into class every week for the pre-class hug. That way he knew to brace himself for equal impact from the brothers.

Daniel and Douglas were enthusiastic in class. They each enjoyed a simple faith that was completely in line with the "right and wrong" emphasis of their developmental stage. In fact, they sometimes functioned as the class policemen.

"Hey, Tommy! You know Mr. Jim doesn't like us wasting the glue making 'second skin' on our fingers! Cut it out!"

"Janet! What's with the face you made to Leo? Doncha know we're in God's house here? We should behave!"

"Marcie, I need to hear the lesson now. Would you please talk to Lucinda after class?"

The boys seemed quite sincere in their attitudes in class. But they never brought stories back about how they were applying their faith outside the church walls. Jim didn't know what to make of it at first. Daniel and Douglas weren't at all shy about speaking up. He was about to call their parents—just to see if anything was making the transfer home from Sunday school—when the Sunday school superintendent called Jim.

"Jim, you have a couple of heroes in your class."

"What do you mean?"

"You have the Johnson boys in your class, right?"

"Daniel and Douglas. Every Sunday, rain or shine."

"Well, get this. They were playing basketball on the church lot when they saw someone crawl into the kitchen window at the church. They saw the pastor's car in his parking space, so they ran to the office to tell him about it. The police came and went into the kitchen. They found one of Daniel's classmates from school stealing food and trying to push the microwave out the window."

"Amazing! Good for them!"

"It doesn't end there. Daniel and Douglas talked to the pastor and the policeman while they were contacting the boy's family. Daniel said, 'We need to put this guy in our Sunday school class.' Douglas followed up. 'Yeah, then he'd learn to do the right thing.' Looks like you'll have another student this Sunday! They're some talkers, you know."

"Do I know! And I was worried about whether what they were learning carried over into the rest of the week."

When the call from the Sunday school superintendent ended, Jim called the boys' mother. "Mrs. Johnson, I just heard about the boys' stopping the burglary at the church. I wanted to call you and tell you how much I appreciate them both."

"Oh, they talk about you all the time. They're always saying something about Sunday school. Just last night they were watching something on TV. Some story where kids were running drugs for a bunch of hoodlums or something. Daniel kept saying, 'No way! No way should those guys be doing that!' And my Douglas said, 'Bet they didn't pay attention in Sunday school.' "

"Could I talk to one of them?"

"If you like, talk to them both. I'll let one of them use the extension in my bedroom."

"That would be great, Mrs. Johnson."

Seconds later, the boys were pouring out their version of the story over the phone. Jim listened with great interest. "Guys, you were great. Thanks for watching out for the church that way. Hey, your mom tells me you're always talking about Sunday school when you're at home. She says you're really good about doing the home part of the lesson. So why don't I ever hear about that the next Sunday?"

Douglas talked first. "You know, Mr. Jim, Daniel and I decided a while back . . ."

And Daniel continued. ". . . that we talked so much during the rest of class that we'd let the other kids cover the first 10 minutes when you ask about the last week. That okay with you?"

Watch This Principle

The principle of transfer bears repeating:

The transfer of a "learned principle" from church to home, or from home to church, cannot be legislated or manipulated—only nurtured.

There's no way to force enthusiasm into faith kids like Daniel and Douglas. But teachers can provide an environment that encourages enthusiasm. As Jim teaches Bible content and helps with application, he works a lot of interaction into his class sessions. The students have opportunities to "get verbal." Jim is a patient teacher. He can walk his class through the general issues that surface if he feels that they are relevant to the majority of the students. He monitors interaction between the students, but he doesn't stifle it very often.

Perhaps most telling in relation to this principle, Jim is an encourager. He sets a tone of encouragement in his classroom, and the students pick up on that attitude. His "can-do" feeling about his students, their ability to learn, and their probable success with the home follow-up each week is clear.

Daniel and Douglas are also blessed with family members who encourage them. Mrs. Johnson is vocal with her praise of them, and she's not afraid to brag on her boys to others even when the boys are close enough to overhear. These two have received so much praise for doing the right thing when they've made good choices that they want to do what's right. "Bringing Sunday school home" has become one of the "right things" they do. So has exercising some of the same respect for "Mr. Jim" as they have for their mother.

So how can you make the most of the transfer principle in the church/home link ?

1) Be a lavish encourager. More than candy, more than carnival prizes, more than bonus points in a contest for a trip to the pizza parlor, simple encouragement is still the best motivator for students. Sure, the rewards are fine once in a while, but they're

not essential. Rewards without vocal encouragement from you can ring hollow; sincere encouragement has a bigger payoff than a hundred candy bars.

2) Help your students make connections between the Bible and everyday life. Yes, your lesson should offer some sort of "life response" exercise each week. But also look for opportunities in class to offer other examples of how the lesson can connect to students' lives outside your classroom. Simple techniques could include quick brainstorming sessions, your own life examples, or even discussing something you read in the paper that week.

3) Encourage students to think through their own ideas about transferring principles from Sunday school to their homes. Even after you've offered your own life example, ask a question like "How do you think you could apply the principle from today's lesson at home? At school?

The reason Daniel and Douglas are so good at making the transfer of principles between Sunday school and home—and back again—is that they've been coached to do just that for years. The principle of transfer may not "take overnight" in your students' growth as faith kids. But when you see it happen, you'll feel one of the most gratifying moments possible as a Faith Teacher.

The Principle
of Appropriateness

11

BIBLICAL LESSONS—WHETHER TAUGHT AT HOME OR IN THE CHURCH—must be age-appropriate and developmentally appropriate for maximum impact on a student.

"Excuse me. Miss Donato?"

"Rex, you are such a gentleman! What can I do for you?"

Rex looked uncomfortable for a moment. Then he straightened his 14-year-old "mall slouch" up into his full height—nearly six feet tall now, Lizi guessed.

"Ma'am, could I get an extra take-home paper this week? I mean, I wouldn't be asking you, but my Dad . . . well . . ."

Lizi's imagination went into hyperdrive. Did Rex's father summarily rip the boy's Sunday school papers into little shreds and consign his son to his room without food for the rest of the day? Did Rex need an extra copy to hide somewhere?

Would this mean an uncomfortable call to a parent she hardly knew?

Someone along the line had taught Rex respect for authority— and manners, for that matter. Rex reflected an "old school" upbringing and spoke in class in ways that led Lizi to believe that his home life, while maybe not Christian, reflected high moral standards.

"What about your dad? Do the papers really bother him or something?"

"Oh, no, ma'am, not at all. In fact, that's the problem. Dad latches on to my Sunday school take-home papers like he latches on to the sports section. If I haven't read it by the time I get home, it's gone until Tuesday—and then I miss the daily devotions part early in the week."

"You mean your father is reading your Sunday school take-home papers?"

"Word for word, ma'am."

"Have I met your father yet? Does he come to church at all?"

"He came to the Christmas program to watch us sing. That's about it."

"Should I ask the pastor to visit him, do you think?"

Rex cocked his head and thought for a moment. "I'm not sure, Miss Donato. See, Dad told me that it was fine with him that I was going to church and bringing my little sister, but that he was an official church dropout."

"Hmm. Well, Rex, I don't see any problem with you taking two papers home with you. Our compliments."

"Thanks, Miss Donato!"

"You know, with each of you having your own copy of the paper, it might make it easier to talk it over with your father. You know, take some time to discuss the stories, maybe even look at some of the Bible passages together."

"Wow, do you think Dad would do that?"

"You won't know until you ask, will you?"

Rex smiled broadly. "The worst he can say is 'no.' All right, I'll give it a try!"

Week after week, Lizi counted out two papers for Rex at the end of class. Week after week, Rex gave her such a look of gratitude that she would have given him another dozen had he asked.

Just seven weeks later, someone showed up at the classroom door with Rex and the pastor. He was the spitting image of Rex, only three inches taller and with a beard.

"Lizi, I want you to meet Robert St. Clair, Rex's father."

"Miss Donato, I'm pleased to meet you. I thought you should meet the recipient of the extra copy of the take-home paper you've been sending home with Rex. We've been talking them over every week.

"It seems that Sunday school has changed since I was a boy. For some reason, the few years I attended did nothing to help me figure out how God fits in with everyday life. We would memorize verses from the Bible in words I couldn't understand, recite theology from creeds that no one explained, and it all took place in a drab room with a stodgy teacher. Nothing like what Rex tells me, or what I see here." Robert motioned to the brightly-colored walls alive with posters and student art.

"But these papers you're sending home—these papers make God make sense. I never had anything explained like this when I was a boy. So I came to talk to the pastor this week, and here I am in church today for the first time in 25 years."

"I'm thrilled you're here, Mr. St. Clair."

"Thank you. May I ask you a favor? I still have a lot of catching up to do. Would you still send home an extra paper with Rex for a while?"

Watch This Principle

Believe it or not, this story reflects the principle of appropriateness: *Biblical lessons—whether taught at home or in the church—must be age-appropriate and developmentally appropriate for maximum impact on a student.*

As he noted, Robert St. Clair had some catching up to do. His faith development had been arrested at the time he left Sunday school as a teen. Therefore, the youth take-home papers that Rex brought home were about right for Robert. Their approach to God and everyday life answered the questions that hadn't been addressed when, in frustration, he had walked out of church 25 years earlier.

But Robert understood that those answers wouldn't be enough

The Principle of Appropriateness

for his adult context. That's why he returned to church—not to attend Rex's class, but an adult class where the issues that face Robert "where he lives" can be covered more fully and appropriately for his adult experience.

To some Christian educators, appropriateness refers to teaching methods. Or it refers to shaping content (reading level, vocabulary, etc.) so that it can be understood and processed at the students' developmental level. But to follow this principle most effectively, we need to apply the appropriateness principle to the content itself. As was the case with Robert, simpler issues and principles might attract an adult for a short while, but if the content fails to speak to the complexity of adult issues, the adult will eventually believe them to be irrelevant—and will tend to believe the same about Sunday school itself.

Let's illustrate with examples from the life of David. David's experiences as a shepherd-poet are attractive to all ages, and rightly so. It would be possible to create a number of lessons with general principles that could work for all ages. Some special curriculums for intergenerational learning do just that.

But such a program is not sustainable throughout the years of Christian education engagement between a church and a student. David's story goes far beyond that of his shepherd years, which are addressed in relatively few chapters of the Scripture. Many more chapters are devoted to his life as a warrior and a king. Those chapters contain accounts of David's failures, including adultery and murder. Therefore, as students mature, they should be exposed to the full witness of David's life—especially those parts of the Bible that they'd have difficulty understanding as children.

A common-content ("uniform") approach to teaching the Bible would likely rob adults of the lessons that could be learned from the full witness of David's life—and the consequent exposure to many chapters of the Bible. It's likely that adults would soon plateau at a simplistic level of understanding. Such a curriculum approach sacrifices the impact of age and developmental appropriateness for a forced uniformity. The result is that the lessons are incomprehensible to some students, and condescending to others.

Would Rex have bothered to take papers home that he thought were boring? Would a thoughtful seeker like Robert be engaged for long in lessons that he found irrelevant to his life as an adult?

We don't think so. That's why the principle of appropriateness matters so much in the church/home link. Here are some appropriateness hints for you:

1) Remember that appropriateness engages both the areas of age and development. This can become a complex principle, but

The Principle of Appropriateness

you can keep it simple by reviewing your curriculum while keeping your students in mind. Is the reading level appropriate for the age? Are the issues relevant to the developmental stage of the students? Is the content approachable for the faith development of the students? Many churches are offering a "seeker's class" during Sunday school as a means to address the initial—and crucial—questions of adults who have no real faith background. This class runs from 3 to 12 months, and helps these seekers become familiar with the basic teachings of Christianity and the Bible itself. It's an option whose time has come.

2) Reshape those sections of your curriculum that don't "fit" well for all of your students. The goal of teaching is to allow God's Word to have maximum impact on your students, not to follow a written lesson to the letter. And here's a secret: Curriculum publishers actually expect you to personalize curriculum! They might be age-level experts, but only you know your students.

3) Periodically ask your students if the material you're using helps them understand God and the Bible better. This assumes, of course, that this is an age-appropriate question for your students. Students are the best reflectors on the curriculum, bar none. Although you likely won't meet their every desire in your Sunday school class, sometimes their comments can help you discover better ways to connect effectively with them. So keep an open ear.

4) Encourage the parents and families of your students to explore age-appropriate material for use at home. They face the same issues regarding appropriateness that you do. You may have

a better understanding of what's available for their use at home simply because you have access to a curriculum catalog—an item which is not in most homes. Offer some suggestions now and then regarding the "best of the best" in faith building on the home front. Most of your parents will appreciate it.

Faith Teachers must recognize both the age and development of the student if the church/home link is to succeed. You may be wondering, "Just how do I do that?"

That's why we're here. The next section of this book will give you a concise and concrete guide to strategies you can use now to succeed in Sunday school—and at home—with almost every age and stage of development in your efforts to "grow" faith kids.

The age-level information in the following section was adapted from the book *Reach Every One You Teach*, by Marlene LeFever, Rosann Englebretson, and Steve Wamberg.

Reach Every One You Teach is published by Cook Communications Ministries.

Toddlers and Two Year Olds

12

Good MORNING, JEREMY!" Melissa, the teacher of toddlers, knelt down and held out her arms. Two-year-old Jeremy ran toward her for a quick hug, then bounced over to his favorite activity center. As Jeremy began piling blocks into the semblance of a wall, Melissa stood and greeted the parents. "Thanks for bringing Jeremy again!"

"He wouldn't let us miss it, even if we wanted to," laughed Mark. "This is one of the highlights of his week."

"I'm glad he feels that way," said Melissa. "And I really appreciate your help, too. Jeremy's really learning a lot."

"How do you know how much he's learning?" asked Kathy. "He seems to forget things quickly, even if we go over the rhymes and songs with him every day."

"That repetition is one of the most important things you can do," Melissa assured them. "Coming here every week makes this classroom feel familiar and safe. He's learning that he can trust me and the teaching assistants. Hearing and doing the same things over and over also makes him feel comfortable and safe. As he hears about God in this safe situation, he'll begin to think of God as someone he can trust. And as he hears the same things at home, that will further strengthen his feeling that he can trust himself to God."

"So you're saying that what he's 'learning' isn't just information. He's learning attitudes about us, about you, about church, and these attitudes lay the foundation for his attitudes toward God."

"That's right." Melissa smiled. "Again, thanks for your help. We've got to work together in order to do this right!"

For two year olds, that's what a successful church/home link looks like. The #1 agenda is *building trust*. What we say to these young children, how we say it, how we treat them, the way we repeat things till they become familiar, the predictable environment we set up for them—all these combine to help the children feel safe and protected. And as they learn to trust us—both parents and teachers—they will be more open to trust God later on.

Toddlers and Two Year Olds

HOW TODDLERS AND TWO YEAR OLDS LEARN

Two year olds are:

1) imitators;

2) experimenters;

3) learning language skills;

4) learning through important relationships; and

5) self-contained (group exercises don't mean as much as individual encounters).

TODDLERS AND TWOS:
WHAT WORKS, WHAT DOESN'T

<u>DO</u>

✔ Create a safe, interesting environment where children can freely explore.

✔ Refer frequently to God, Jesus, and the Bible to lay a solid foundation for future spiritual growth.

✔ Create an emotionally warm environment that builds trust.

✔ Present Bible stories in brief, short presentations, encouraging movement and participation by the children.

✔ Encourage lots of talking and repeating.

✔ Teach children individually or in small groups.

✔ Encourage crafts and projects which allow children to enjoy the process of creating.

DON'T

✗ Don't have any unsafe conditions which would keep the children from moving safely about.

✗ Don't assume that toddlers are too young to be exposed to Bible truths.

✗ Don't tell lengthy Bible stories as children sit passively.

✗ Don't discourage children from talking and interacting.

✗ Don't teach the whole class at one time if the class is large.

✗ Don't pass out class activities which require coloring in lines or in which all the crafts look exactly the same when finished.

Preschoolers (3–5 Years)

13

"WHY IS GOD A BIRD?"

The question alarmed Steffi. What had she done to confuse little Lori so much?

"Honey, God isn't a bird." But the preschool class time was over, and Steffi was left stewing about what might have produced such a notion, in Lori..

Thankfully, Lori's mother Tess was in frequent communication with Steffi about Lori's Christian education.

"Guess what question Lori asked on the way home from church?"

"The same one she asked me at the end of class: Why is God a bird?"

"Ah, she asked you the same question! Well, I had to follow up on that. I asked her what she learned in Sunday school this morning. She said, 'I learned about the Holy Parrot.' "

"The Holy Parrot?"

"You know, Steffi, she heard you talk about the dove coming down from heaven and the Holy Spirit. Her mind made the jump from that conversation to her favorite bird at the pet shop: that pretty parrot in the front window. The result was the 'Holy Parrot.' "

"Tell you what. I'll review this lesson next Sunday just to make sure we don't have pet shop deities in the minds of any other kids.

"Is Lori still wondering why God is a bird?"

"We're still working on that. I think that review could help."

Sometimes building faith kids means keeping the content responsive to the needs of your students.

HOW PRESCHOOLERS LEARN

Preschoolers' brains are hungry for input from a variety of sources. That's why they love the question "Why?" so much. Preschoolers are:

1) questioners;

2) able to focus on only one aspect of a situation at a time;

3) sensory learners;

4) able to do many more things physically than toddlers and twos;

5) group learners; and

6) roaming learners.

PRESCHOOLERS:
WHAT WORKS, WHAT DOESN'T

<u>DO</u>

- ✔ Tell the Bible story with the Bible open at the appropriate passage to reinforce the fact that the stories come from the Bible and that they are true.
- ✔ Provide activities that allow children to use their large muscle skills.
- ✔ Offer choices of activities—varied learning centers with options that use as many of their senses as possible.
- ✔ Provide opportunities for children to practice their developing finger dexterity skills such as cutting, coloring, sorting, and stringing.
- ✔ Have creative play experiences—roleplaying, dramatization, music, and movement.
- ✔ Allow their expanding vocabularies to be stretched through small-group discussions and shared projects.
- ✔ Encourage their natural curiosity by valuing their questions.

<u>DON'T</u>

- ✘ Don't concentrate so much on making the Bible stories entertaining that the children miss the point that the stories come from the Bible, which comes from God.
- ✘ Don't expect preschool children to sit quietly for long periods of time.
- ✘ Don't have only one activity for all children.

✘ Don't give preschoolers craft activities where the adult has done most of the work and the children merely do the assembly.

✘ Don't expect preschool children to be the audience and not the participants.

✘ Don't be the one to always do all the talking.

✘ Don't discourage or ignore the constant "whys" you will hear.

Early Elementary Children

14

MAGGIE TOOK THE DOLL AND PUT IT CAREFULLY IN A BOX in the corner of the classroom.

"Baby Jesus is sleeping now." Maggie carefully covered up the doll with a small cloth.

"Then we need shepherds and sheep." Erin was telling the Christmas story and having the children act it out as she went along. "Who can be a good sheep and make the sounds that go with it? Who can be nice shepherds?"

After three "sheep" volunteered and bleated, two first graders took their places beside them. "Now the angels have a very important announcement. Who's ready to make that announcement?"

Jake volunteered. "Okay, Jake, stand near the shepherds and repeat after me: Behold!"

"What?"

"Behold!"

" 'Big hole'? What's a big hole have to do with Jesus getting born?"

"Never mind, Jake. You'll understand when you read the story yourself next year. Just tell the shepherds that God has great news waiting for them in Bethlehem—it's a baby in a manger!"

"God has great news for you—a baby in a manger! Over there in the corner!"

"Jake! This corner is Bethlehem, remember?" Maggie wanted everyone to remember that point.

Erin loved the Christmas story anyway, and she loved it even more today because every child could easily take a part in it. These children were natural actors—at least at this stage in their development.

For early elementary students, simple dramas like this are one of the best group learning experiences that could be offered.

HOW EARLY ELEMENTARY CHILDREN LEARN

Early elementary students (kindergarten and first grade) are:

    1) dramatists and roleplayers;

    2) hands-on creators;

    3) simple, focused, concrete thinkers; and

    4) almost consumed by the process of learning to read.

Early Elementary Children

EARLY ELEMENTARY CHILDREN:
WHAT WORKS, WHAT DOESN'T

<u>DO</u>

- ✔ Establish eye contact with the children and smile.
- ✔ Provide reading material that is a match for their reading abilities.
- ✔ Encourage students to show that they know exactly what the Bible story is about by retelling the Bible content using dramatization, puppets, or role-playing.
- ✔ Promote interactive creativity by providing activity choices which include cutting, constructing, and creating.
- ✔ Encourage activities that match the learning of new readers—recognizing letters, frequent writing opportunities, repetitive text to read.
- ✔ Recognize that the most important book these children will ever be exposed to is the Bible.

<u>DON'T</u>

- ✘ Don't underestimate what children will pick up from your facial expressions.
- ✘ Don't expect most of the children to be able to read complex material.
- ✘ Don't assume children have understood the Bible content simply because the story is finished.

✗ Don't pass out worksheets to early elementary students which require no interaction, activity, or response.

✗ Don't ignore the fact that learning to read is a consuming part of their lives.

✗ Don't miss opportunities to relate their new reading abilities to a future of reading the Bible.

Elementary Children

15

EIGHT-YEAR-OLD CHRISTOPHER WAS A REALITY TESTER. Every idea that came up in Sunday school class was put under scrutiny.

"That doesn't sound right." That simple statement would send the class off on a discussion about what was real and what wasn't, what was true and false, what was right and wrong.

The kids in Janice's class completely loved reality testing. But Janice often wondered how much of that testing happened outside Sunday school, and how much was being done "just for her benefit."

A few days ago, Christopher's father, Ralph, stopped Janice at a church fellowship coffee. "Janice, I think you'll enjoy this. Christopher and I were watching a TV program sympathetic to a cult the other night. Christopher kept saying, 'That doesn't sound right. That isn't true. That's not true.'

"He kept at it for so long that I finally asked him, 'Christopher, how do you know what they believe and do isn't true?'

"Know what he said? 'Dad, when you've been in Sunday school as many years as I have, you know what's right and what's wrong.' You know, he's in a stage of testing everything these days. I'm just glad he's testing what he hears on TV, too."

Janice smiled. "Me, too."

Faith kids need standards to "test the waters" of what they hear in everyday life. The elementary school age is a prime age developmentally to encourage that kind of testing.

HOW ELEMENTARY CHILDREN LEARN

Elementary children (second and third graders) share these characteristics:

1) logical thinking;

2) a love for facts;

3) demonstrated reasoning and sorting skills;

4) a sense of "right and wrong" justice; and

5) cooperation with common group goals.

ELEMENTARY CHILDREN:
WHAT WORKS, WHAT DOESN'T

<u>DO</u>

- ✔ Work hard to catch every child being good and make a big deal of it.
- ✔ Have opportunities for group projects, activities, and interaction.
- ✔ Provide as much factual and background information as you can when presenting the Bible story.
- ✔ Encourage students to use their Bibles to find verses and references.
- ✔ Allow students to make choices between activities.
- ✔ Enjoy the corny jokes and puns of elementary students.

<u>DON'T</u>

- ✘ Don't simply discipline bad or annoying behavior.
- ✘ Don't require the children to sit quietly and do all work individually throughout the class.
- ✘ Don't present Bible stories without giving some sort of context for the stories.
- ✘ Don't tell the students about the Bible content without allowing them the chance to look up verses themselves.
- ✘ Don't have students do the same thing throughout the lesson.
- ✘ Don't expect sophisticated humor or adult thinking.

Upper Elementary Children

16

W ho's this, Mrs. Tennant?" asked Peter.

"This is Martin. He's new in town, and his family has decided to come to our church."

"Oh." Then Peter was off to talk to a friend.

It wasn't as though Martin had five eyes showing or anything. Still, Betty had to remind herself that fourth and fifth graders were very group-conscious. She'd have to remind them to open their group to Martin.

"Stuart, will you come here for a minute?"

Stuart was one of the leaders among the kids. "Hi, Mrs. Tennant. What's up?"

"Stuart, this is Martin. He came with his family to church today. They're new in town. Will you introduce him around to the rest of the class before we start today?"

Stuart looked Martin over. Then he stuck out his hand. "I'm Stuart. Do you play soccer?"

Martin relaxed a bit and nodded. "Yeah. Usually goalie. I'm Martin."

Stuart turned around and said to everyone within hearing, "Hey guys, come meet Martin! He can play goalie! He's here with his family today. They're all new in town, and they're at our church!"

Faith kids can bond together and form strong groups. At this age, those groups can become almost exclusionary of others. But often it doesn't take much for faith kids to reach outside their group when they're encouraged to do so.

HOW UPPER ELEMENTARY STUDENTS LEARN

These characteristics describe your upper elementary (fourth and fifth grade) students:

1) an emphasis on group membership;

2) ability to analyze facts and intentions;

3) logical thinking;

4) a love for facts;

5) demonstrated logic and sorting skills;

6) a strong sense of "right and wrong" justice; and

7) cooperation with common group goals.

UPPER ELEMENTARY CHILDREN:
WHAT WORKS, WHAT DOESN'T

<u>DO</u>

- ✔ Provide opportunities for students to study the Bible and look up verses, references, and passages.
- ✔ Encourage acceptance of all God's children—vary the seating frequently.
- ✔ Allow students to come to group consensus about class-room rules.
- ✔ Provide opportunities for cooperative group work as well as independent study.
- ✔ Allow students to make choices between activities.
- ✔ Keep classroom instruction as concrete and experiential as possible.

<u>DON'T</u>

- ✘ Don't tell the students all the Bible content as they passively listen.
- ✘ Don't allow students to sit in cliques or always with the same peers.
- ✘ Don't present a set of rules to follow and exclude students from having input.
- ✘ Don't only have students work individually on projects and activities.
- ✘ Don't have students do the same thing for the whole lesson.
- ✘ Don't present abstract concepts like "witnessing" without concrete examples and roleplaying practice.

Middle Schoolers

17

Eric COULDN'T BELIEVE HIS EYES when he walked into his Sunday school classroom that fall. What had happened to all those nice, compact sixth graders?

Some of them had been replaced by other nice, compact sixth graders. Others had morphed into much taller students.

"Wow, have you guys changed!"

"So has school, Mr. Barnes." Ricky was a sixth grader. "We have to switch classes every 45 minutes now."

"Yeah, and we aren't the pond scum of the school anymore!" Sean was a confident eighth grader who was sure to enjoy his turn at the top of the middle school totem pole.

"My friends are all in different groups this year." Kenny was pretty reflective for a seventh grader. "They're all dividing up between athletes, preps, and brains. They make me feel like I have to decide on one group, too. But I don't want to."

"My parents still won't let me date—and I'm almost 14!" Laura was ready to make her social crisis the issue of the day.

"You know, in all this change, God is still consistent." With that, Eric called the class to order—and another year of building faith kids was on its way.

Faith kids need to learn how to deal with change—and nowhere is that change as dramatic as in the middle school years. A calling to teach this age is a calling to real adventure!

HOW MIDDLE SCHOOLERS LEARN

Change is the definitive word for middle schoolers (sixth, seventh and eighth graders), who share these characteristics:

1) dealing with change in school buildings, routines, and friends;

2) a profound emphasis on peer relationships;

3) physical changes (both visible and internal);

4) a gradual shift from concrete to abstract thinking; and

5) the ability to reflect on one's own thoughts and actions.

MIDDLE SCHOOLERS:
WHAT WORKS, WHAT DOESN'T

DO

- ✔ Allow for plenty of group interaction time, with partners, small groups, or with the whole group.
- ✔ Create an atmosphere where every student is valued and included—encourage acceptance of all.
- ✔ Set up opportunities for active games and team activities.
- ✔ Encourage the exchange of ideas and much discussion— find out what they're thinking.
- ✔ Allow students to make choices between activities; balance competitive and noncompetitive activities.
- ✔ Pose challenging questions that expand the students' thinking.
- ✔ Help the students understand the symbolism and truths represented in proverbs and parables.
- ✔ Encourage students to choose to make a plan to apply what they learned during the week.

DON'T

- ✘ Don't have students work only independently.
- ✘ Don't allow students to sit in cliques or always with the same peers; don't embarrass students for any reason.
- ✘ Don't rely on seatwork for the entire class period.
- ✘ Don't do all the talking and expect students to listen.
- ✘ Don't have the students do the same thing the whole time.
- ✘ Don't give students all the answers.

✘ Don't expect every middle school student to fully understand figurative language.

✘ Don't dictate to students how to use what they have learned.

High Schoolers

HOW DO YOU DEFINE YOURSELF?

Butch knew it was a question that most of his high school students worked with every day. He also knew it was a question many of their parents had never really resolved.

He listened to his class week after week. He listened to some of his students identify themselves with phrases like "I'm ugly." "I'm stupid." "I'm lazy."

And he knew those descriptions weren't true.

Then there were all the group descriptions: "preppies," "skaters," "ravers," "kickers," and several others he'd never heard of before.

The high schoolers were looking for someone or something to identify with. Butch's goal for them was as simple as it was profound: to have each student in the class find his or her primary identity as a child of God through a relationship with Jesus.

Then the rest of their identity could fall into place.

Faith kids in high school are seeking an identity. If you offer a strong and compelling Sunday school experience, you can have a significant impact on their search—and earn the lasting gratitude of your faith growth partners (their parents) in the process.

HOW HIGH SCHOOLERS LEARN

These characteristics mark a student's high school years:

    1) the search for, and establishment of, personal identity;

    2) the profound influence of peers; and

    3) the continued shift toward abstract thinking.

These characteristics reflect a maturing process that enables a search for values.

HIGH SCHOOLERS:
WHAT WORKS, WHAT DOESN'T
<u>DO</u>

✔ Expect your students to challenge values and beliefs. Create a place where questioning is "safe."

✔ Encourage discussion one-on-one, with small groups or as a whole class.

✔ Challenge your students to discover what is important to them.

High Schoolers

✔ Set up opportunities for active games and team activities.

✔ Encourage the exchange of ideas and much discussion—
find out what they are thinking.

✔ Allow students to make choices between activities.

✔ Provide activities to encourage group problem solving.

✔ Expose your students to moral reasoning and biblical values.

✔ Encourage students to make a plan to apply what they
learned to their lives.

✔ Be a powerful, positive role model.

DON'T

✘ Don't discourage "big" questions.

✘ Don't lecture exclusively.

✘ Don't assume all students know what is important.

✘ Don't rely on seatwork for the entire class period.

✘ Don't do all the talking and expect students to only listen.

✘ Don't have students do the same thing for the entire lesson.

✘ Don't give students all the answers.

✘ Don't hesitate to challenge students to think about their
own moral beliefs.

✘ Don't dictate to students how to apply what they have
learned.

✘ Don't underestimate the impact you're having on students.

Adults

Gene was ready to cocoon. He was tired of all the hassle of getting up on Sunday morning, getting the kids ready, and getting to church.

He wanted time to himself. He was ready to fall asleep to one of those boring news analysis shows. He wanted to be in front of the TV in time for a Sunday afternoon kickoff for once.

If he was going to be active on this beautiful autumn morning, he wanted to walk down to the neighborhood coffee shop and order a double espresso with hazelnut syrup and a German pastry guaranteed to melt in his mouth. He wanted God to meet him at the park and talk over life issues instead of having to deal with all the pseudo-political concerns of who was wearing what and which visitor had violated a family's designated pew.

Today, Gene wanted the answers to his life issues on a billboard; enough of this searching stuff. He wanted his wife and kids to be happy. He wanted his dad to be alive again for one more round of golf. He wanted the shape that faced him in the mirror to be thinner right now. He wanted to run the winning touchdown of his last high school game all over again.

But he got up and dressed for church anyway. After all, he was the teacher of the adult Sunday school class.

When faith kids become adults, they have to deal with "real life" as never before. Sometimes that real life is so consuming and tiring that they just want to shut themselves off for awhile. It's called "cocooning," and it's a regular phenomenon even among Christians these days. Still, God's Word stands as the standard for church and home during the adult years—and if you're teaching adults, you know you're engaged in a variety of life's big issues in response to their needs.

HOW ADULTS LEARN

Adults' lives are marked by:

1) transitions;
2) family involvement; and
3) vocational concerns.

The more relevant your class can be in making God's Word connect with the lives of your students, the greater impact you'll have.

ADULTS:

WHAT WORKS, WHAT DOESN'T

DO

✔ Create a sense of community.

✔ Gear the format of your class around discussion and idea exchange.

✔ Help adults see the relevance of what is being learned. Connect the content of the lesson with everyday life.

✔ Provide choices for learning activities.

✔ Cover topics that Christians face at any age; understand the differences between adult generations.

✔ Honor the unique learning styles of individual adults.

✔ Offer a time for students to determine a strategy of personal application of the lesson content during the week.

DON'T

✘ Don't provide only individual study opportunities.

✘ Don't lecture exclusively.

✘ Don't teach the content and facts without applications.

✘ Don't have the class do the same thing the whole time.

✘ Don't underestimate the value of adult generations learning from one another.

✘ Don't assume that all adults learn the same.

✘ Don't dictate to the students how to apply the lesson to their lives.

Keep On Keeping On 20

"We are here today to commission David Anderson as a short-term missionary . . . ."

Sarah had known David "when." Twenty years ago, she'd taught David's early elementary Sunday school class. As a boy, David was usually all over the classroom. Sarah was almost surprised that he could stay still on the platform as the pastor laid his hands on David to pray.

Sarah scanned the room. There at the front of the sanctuary were seven young adults who had been David's classmates then—some with their own families now. Sarah had been able to teach 14 early elementary children, then move up with them as they got older—all the way into their teen years. She'd been on the retreat where most of them made commitments to serve Jesus—and every one of them had delivered on that commitment.

Not every one of them was in professional ministry. Three were pastors, one was a full-time missionary. The others were like David: looking to serve Jesus with their everyday skills and talents. David was trained as an engineer. He was about to take a design for an irrigation system with him overseas and implement it while he shared the Gospel.

Three others of David's classmates were on the platform with him. The others? They were serving somewhere and couldn't make it back for this service. But Sarah wouldn't have missed it for the world—and will tell you in a heartbeat why she's still teaching Sunday school.

You have everything you need to make the church/home link between your Sunday school class and your students' homes succeed. You had what you needed before you picked up this book. We hope that this book gave you a few new ideas about using what you have.

Your partners in this endeavor are God and the parents of the children you teach.

Your tools to make the church/home link work include a "need-content-application-response" lesson at church, its application at home, and your follow-up when the students return to your classroom.

Your strategies to make the most of the church/home link include the following principles:

Content. The content of teaching must support its application.

Context. Christian education strategies—at church and home—must address the fullest context of the student's life. Therefore, they must complement each other.

Focus. The focus of a Sunday school lesson is the impact of God's Word on groups of individuals; the target for content is the common ground shared by students at a certain developmental stage. The focus of a home lesson is the impact of God's Word on an individual; the target for content is what uniquely suits one person. When both church and home keep their focus, students can focus too.

Location. Location—church or home—helps determine the most effective approach for Christian education strategy.

Connectivity. The church and home are inherently connected by a well-executed "need-content-application-response" lesson at church, its application at home, and the student's return to church for accountability and reinforcement. Work this feedback loop for all it's worth.

Maturation. Each student will mature in a unique way, not in lockstep with other students. Maturation involves more than "head knowledge," too. It encompasses every aspect of a person's life development.

Humanity. The goal of Christian teaching, whether at church or at home, is to put a human voice to God's Word and a human model to God's ways.

Transfer. The transfer of a "learned principle" from church to home, or from home to church, cannot be legislated or manipulated—only nurtured.

Appropriateness. Biblical lessons—whether taught at home or in the church—must be age-appropriate and developmentally appropriate for maximum impact on a student.

Your filters for analyzing curriculum are age-appropriateness, developmental appropriateness, and the "need-content-application-response" structure.

Your goal, with God's help, is to grow faith kids.

Now you know who they are. Do you understand how significant you are?

You're a teacher. You're among the rare breed Henry Adams referred to when he observed, "A teacher affects eternity; no one can tell where his influence stops."

More than that, you're a Faith Teacher. Faith Teaching is the process the church uses to develop faith kids by helping them learn and apply Bible truth to their lives. This teaching usually follows an intentional plan and takes place in a more structured environment than the home.

Keep On Keeping On

Nowhere is the eternal effect of teaching more pronounced than in a Sunday school classroom. If you believe God's Word, you know your content and its application can save lives—now and forever.

At the same time, you're a faith kid yourself. You allow Jesus Christ to show in your words and deeds wherever you go—including your classroom.

You've been doing that for years, too. So keep doing what you've been doing—only better. Use the link that already exists between church and home for the sake of the students you serve. As one of over 4 million Sunday school teachers serving over 30 million students today, teach the faith.

And keep it too.